Introduction to

Christian Faith

A Deeper Way of Seeing

NEAL F. FISHER

Introduction to Christian Faith: A Deeper Way of Seeing

The General Board of Higher Education and Ministry leads and serves The United Methodist Church in the recruitment, preparation, nurture, education, and support of Christian leaders—lay and clergy—for the work of making disciples of Jesus Christ for the transformation of the world. Its vision is that a new generation of Christian leaders will commit boldly to Jesus Christ and be characterized by intellectual excellence, moral integrity, spiritual courage, and holiness of heart and life. The General Board of Higher Education and Ministry of The United Methodist Church serves as an advocate for the intellectual life of the church. The Board's mission embodies the Wesleyan tradition of commitment to the education of laypersons and ordained persons by providing access to higher education for all persons.

Wesley's Foundery Books is named for the abandoned foundery that early followers of John Wesley transformed into a church, which became the cradle of London's Methodist movement.

Introduction to Christian Faith: A Deeper Way of Seeing

{ *For Elaine and LilaLee* }

Contents

CONTENTS

Acknowledgments

It is a pleasant responsibility to say thanks to many friends and colleagues who have contributed thoughtfully in the preparation of this book. Jack Seymour conferred helpfully with me at the beginning of the project, and he later read a draft of the book and gave valuable counsel and suggestions for its refinement. Marjorie Eckhardt read the manuscript and gave careful attention to proper form and clarity throughout. Lallene Rector provided both her personal interest in the project and her strong support in seeing it through to publication. Adolf Hansen made thoughtful suggestions on the organization of the book and gave a critical reading to parts of the manuscript that related to events in the life of his family. Sue D'Alessio likewise read and commented helpfully on a section of the book that referred to events arising from her pastoral ministry.

Jack Bremer, Ardis Chapman, Clarke Chapman, Harold Garman, and Hendrik Pieterse have reviewed all or portions of the manuscript and shared helpful responses. I am indebted to members of my immediate and extended family for reading and charitably responding to what I have written. They include: Gregory Fisher, the Nicholas Lodge and Bryn Fisher family, the Kirk Fisher and Sharon McManus family, AvaJo Shippy, and Tara Walzel.

I have discussed portions of the book with members of several congregations at which I have preached while I was preparing this work, and I have been fortified by their interest and support. Kathryn Armistead, publisher for Foundery Books, has been a valuable guide and colleague in preparing the book, and I have been grateful to benefit from her knowledge and experience in seeing it through to publication. For all those, named and unnamed, who have shown interest and given support, I am deeply grateful.

While discussing Christian faith always requires our best thinking, it is never merely an academic exercise. Faith is related to all we experience and undergo. Ten years ago I experienced the loss of Ila, my wife and companion of fifty years, after her courageous and extended struggle with debilitating illness. I dedicated an earlier book to her. Several months following Ila's death, my younger sister, Elaine McBride, was diagnosed with an aggressive form of cancer that eventually claimed her life. We talked during the months of Elaine's declining health about faith and trust in God both in life and in death, and she gave luminous witness to her faith both in her congregation and in individual conversations. I shared then my intent to write a book interpreting how it is that we are found in faith and place our trust in God. LilaLee had walked a similar path as she cared for her late husband through a long terminal illness and also lost a brother through death. Together we discovered that a new relationship could take root and flourish even in the shadow of mourning and loss. We have cause every day to give thanks for a marriage that has brought love, blessing, and joy into our lives. Her interest and support in writing about faith have been invaluable. This book is for Elaine and LilaLee.

Preface

For now, we see in a mirror,
dimly, but then we will see face to face.
Now I know only in part; then I will know fully,
even as I have been fully known.

—1 Corinthians 13:12

Many believe in God—or struggle to believe—but wonder how it is possible to truly know the divine. How can our limited minds grasp what is ultimately real? Do our religious views represent anything more than vain wishes or subjective imagination? How can we know?

Knowing and experiencing God is not an abstract theory but an intensely personal issue. By confronting the genuine joys we experience, and the agony and sorrows we endure, in faith we can reach out to connect our lives with a source of meaning, an object of devotion that will anchor our lives in something more lasting than ourselves.

To have faith in anything, we must depend on things we cannot prove, whether in religion or in science. Faith in God is a decision to act on the conviction that certain things are true and will be shown at last to be so. Convictions grow out of events and traditions found to be particularly transparent to Ultimate Reality, to

God. Becoming a Christian is embracing the Christian story as the story of our lives and the disclosure of who we are and to whom we belong. The gifts of faith, hope, and love are deeper ways of seeing and responding to the presence of God in our daily lives. They refract the light of life in our spirits and equip us to sense God in, with, and beyond the world that God has made. Those who love are from God and know God. And the love of God never ends.

In this book we will consider how it is that humans come to faith in God and how this faith is confirmed in life. We will also compare and contrast attitudes toward science and religious faith and show how these ways of knowing complement one another rather than compete. Science and religion are different ways of seeing, speaking about, and experiencing our world. We will show how each can illuminate the other.

Recent changes in scientific worldviews and in religious thought provide a new and promising opportunity to consider our faith in God. Some skeptical viewpoints on the question are shaped largely by assumptions arising out of the eighteenth century and the science of that era. Many Enlightenment thinkers concluded that real knowledge of the world comes primarily through what we can measure and observe. In that view values and religious faith are opinions that inform us not about the objective world but solely about the subjective states of the individuals holding them.

Recent best sellers by writers such as Richard Dawkins, Christopher Hitchens, and others embody these assumptions. Like many, they disparage religious faith of any kind and promote a form of atheism they believe is supported by their scientific findings. Yet they too have faith. They have faith that science is the sole source of knowledge of the real world. Other sources of knowledge, they suggest, are delusions or pathetic attempts to escape the realities of the real world. In their view the world and human life within it are products solely of randomized chance and are fully determined by natural forces and drives.

Theology has long contended with these challenges and other deeply rooted forms of atheism in the writings of Ludwig Feuerbach, Sigmund Freud, and Karl Marx. In some instances, the Christian response has been a form of fundamentalism or fideism. More recently it has taken the form of "radical orthodoxy." Some have sought to defend Christian faith by holding to a view of biblical inerrancy. At the other extreme are forms of Christian theology that accept the basic elements of the Enlightenment perspective and attempt to show how the Christian message can be accommodated to that view of the world.

This book is an introduction to faith, and it promotes the idea that Christians can be both thinking and faithful people. Reading it will help you understand how faith is fashioned from our most basic convictions about what is real and true. At its most basic level, faith speaks of that to which we ultimately give ourselves, and its intent is to guide us toward what is beyond—beyond us—our imagining, our time, and our world.

Faith and the Search for God

The danger is not lest the soul should doubt
whether there is any bread,
but lest, by a lie,
it should persuade itself that it is not hungry.

—Simone Weil

As a deer longs for flowing streams,
*   so my soul longs for you, O God.*
My soul thirsts for God,
*   for the living God.*
When shall I come and behold
*   the face of God?*
My tears have been my food
*   day and night,*
while people say to me continually,
*   "Where is your God?"*

—Psalm 42:1-3

Mary Anne Evans, writing in nineteenth-century England under the pen name of George Eliot, was not always on easy terms with the established Church of England. Yet in her novel *Adam Bede* she shows a firm grasp of the meaning of faith. Some of the best lines in the novel were given to a character named Dinah. Dinah was a Free Church preacher who preached the gospel in the open fields and the village commons of the English countryside. In one of the scenes of the novel, Dinah brings her message home in these terms: "Ah, dear friends, we are in sad want of good news about God. And what does other good news signify if we haven't that? For everything else comes to an end and when we die we shall leave it all, but God lasts when everything else is gone. What shall we do if God is not our friend?"[1]

Dinah was not sophisticated as measured by years of schooling, but in her sermons she connected profoundly with her hearers and displayed a deep understanding of the faith she proclaimed. Her outdoor congregations understood that life was a fleeting gift that would one day be withdrawn. Dinah commended to them a trust and reliance upon the One who "lasts when everything else is gone." What tidings could surpass the knowledge that the God who endures was also their eternal friend?

Yearning for God[2]

George Eliot's preacher, Dinah, was touching on a need that reaches far more widely than rural England and lasts long after

---

1   This quote was first brought to my attention by Ernest T. Campbell in "The Fall and Rise of Preaching," The Heim Memorial Lecture, *Aware*, Spring/Summer, 1984.

2   This heading is the title of a study by Margaret Ann Crain and Jack Seymour, *Yearning for God: Reflections of Faithful Lives* (Nashville: Upper Room Books, 2003).

the close of the nineteenth century. The search for God or for god is fixed in human experience. Failing to find God, we will invest our energies on objects of devotion of our own making, thinking thereby to fortify ourselves and find permanence amid the perishing of all that we hold dear.

The psalm writer compares our desire for God with the urgency of a deer, parched with thirst, looking for the refreshment of cool, flowing streams. Our witness in Psalm 42 speaks of sleepless nights attended by tears as he seeks God. In the fourth century, Saint Augustine wrote in his *Confessions*: "Thou movest us in delight in praising Thee; for Thou hast formed us for Thyself, and our hearts are restless until they find rest in Thee."[3]

> The search for God is about more than religion.

Dinah says that other good news means nothing if we lack good news from God. A philosopher from the last century, Alfred North Whitehead, put it in contrasting form. Religion, he said, "is the vision of something that stands beyond, behind, and within, the passing flux of immediate things, something that is real, and yet waiting to be realized, something that is a remote possibility and yet the greatest of present facts, something whose possession is the final good, and yet is beyond reach; something that is the ultimate ideal and the hopeless quest."[4]

---

3   Saint Augustine, *The Confessions*, ed. Whitney J. Oates, *Basic Writings of Saint Augustine* (New York: Random House, 1948), 1:1.

4   Alfred North Whitehead, *Science and the Modern World*, 228 (1933 ed.), quoted in Ian T. Ramsey, *Christian Discourse: Some Logical Explorations* (London: Oxford University, 1965), 66.

The quest for God is a religious question, but the search for God is not confined to religion narrowly defined. We see a kindred venture in the quest to identify the permanent in the midst of the changing. Science, for example, searches for elegant principles that accurately describe the cosmos. Marcelo Gleiser, physicist and astronomer, sums up some of the leading current theories on the formation of the universe as it is understood in scientific circles. He refers to the discovery of cosmic microwave background radiation that is distributed uniformly and now is understood as a residue from the "big bang" with which the universe began 13.7 billion years ago. He notes the instantaneous inflation of the universe and its continuing expansion at an accelerating rate, as well as the formation of our solar system about 5 billion years ago. As Gleiser concludes his summary, he refers to efforts to understand not only *that* the universe meets the incredibly fine tolerances that are essential for the formation of human life, but also *why* and *how* those tolerances were formed. What separates us from God, he concludes, is "our finite life span, the fact that our bodies perish in time. . . . We exist in time, whereas God exists without." He continues:

> Our yearning for a unified theory could not have evolved outside a religious culture deeply influenced by monotheism. . . . The pursuit of an all-encompassing theory, rational and technical as it is, is also the passionate pursuit of something much larger than ourselves, something timeless, universal, all-determining.[5]

---

5   Marcelo Gleiser, *The Prophet and the Astronomer: A Scientific Journey to the End of Time* (New York: W. W. Norton, 2001), 234.

Gleiser, of course, is not alone in sensing the scientific quest as one that is harmonious with the religious quest for God. Stephen Hawking, while not identifying himself as a person of religious faith, alludes to a stance not unlike faith when he writes about the formation of the universe. He speaks of our desire to know not only the underlying order of the world but also to answer the question "why we are here and where we came from."[6] Through the course of the discussion, he holds to the hope of discovering a unified theory that can explain why we and the universe exist. "If we find the answer to that," he concludes at the end of his book, "it would be the ultimate triumph of human reason—for then we would know the mind of God."[7]

To cite these highly varied expressions of the quest for God is, of course, not to suggest that the poet of Psalm 42 and the physicist of the twenty-first century are identifying what they mean by "God" in the same way. For the psalmist, and perhaps for us as well, the God we are seeking is an answer to a deep and personal spiritual concern rather than an inclusive "theory of everything," as the scientists refer to it. It does suggest, however, that faith begins as an attempt to relate to the widest context, the most enduring basis of our lives. And the conviction of faith, it should be added, is that the God who is the enduring Source of our lives is also the One who is seeking us. "Thou hast formed us for Thyself, and our hearts are restless until they find their rest in Thee."

———————————————

6   Stephen Hawking, *A Brief History of Time: From the Big Bang to Black Holes* (New York: Bantam Books, 1988), 3.
7   Ibid., 175.

Faith, God, and Idols

We are therefore raising the question of God as it actually confronts us, that is, as an intensely personal issue, not as a theory on the formation of the universe. Confronting the genuine joy we experience and the agony and sorrow we endure, we reach out to connect our lives with a source of meaning, an object of devotion that will anchor our lives in something more lasting than ourselves.

It is well to ask ourselves what it is that gives meaning and standing in our lives. Of course there are family and work responsibilities that require our attention. But beyond that, what are the elements of our lives that summon our devotion? For what would we like to be remembered? Whatever our stage of life, what would we like inscribed on our gravestones or written in our obituaries? When we are honest with ourselves, we have to admit to a whole constellation of objects or causes with which we would like to be identified and to which we give our energies. Many people will find their jobs, their trades, or their professions as a central focus for their lives. They will regard their standing in those callings and their attainment as a consuming passion. Others will divide their attentions equally between work and family. For some the focus will be on a home, a car, or other possessions, which will mark them as successful and convey status and worth.

But perhaps the most common consuming passion is wealth, not just enough money to sustain life and provide for health and education. Wealth itself can be a consuming and unquenchable thirst. For example, a wealthy man of retirement age sat in his penthouse office in a Midwestern city and told his friend of many years about his family life. He said that his wife was ill, so she had to live several hundred miles away in a warmer, Southern climate. His friend responded bluntly, "George, you already have more money than you could spend in two lifetimes. Why in heaven's name don't you give up this job and move to live out your retirement years with your wife?" George responded: "I'm in this game, and in this game they keep score with money." Money and the acquisition of great amounts of it constituted his way of making a name for himself, "winning the game," and thus establishing, he thought, a legacy. He thought he had money. The money, in fact, had him.

The sad fact is that all of our attainments and accomplishments, whether selfish or noble in their own right, will one day come to an end. Our possessions will corrode and crumble. Our trophies and plaques will gather dust in an attic. Even our best efforts, worthy and laudable though they may be, will not endure. For some this recognition leads to despair. At the beginning of the twentieth century, Bertrand Russell took the very long view and wrote, "All the labours of the ages, all the devotion, all the inspiration, all the noonday brightness of human genius, are destined to extinction in the vast death of the solar system, and . . . the whole temple of Man's achievement must inevitably be buried beneath the debris of a universe in ruins."[8]

While most of us will not succumb to such grandiloquent despair, we are nonetheless sobered by the sheer transitory nature of life and all our accomplishments. In terms of faith, the means by which we seek to fortify our standing in the midst of

---

8   Bertrand Russell, "A Free Man's Worship" (1903), quoted in Robert John Russell, "Cosmology, Creation, and Contingency," in *Cosmos as Creation: Theology and Science in Consonance,* ed. Ted Peters (Nashville: Abingdon Press, 1989), 201.

change may be read as a form of our search for God. Martin Luther said that those objects in which we place our trust and reliance constitute our idols, our gods. "For the two, faith and God, hold close together. Whatever then thy heart clings to . . . and relies upon, that is properly thy God."[9] In Luther's terms, then, whatever we depend on for our worth and standing is in some fashion a god to us. Put in this way, we can understand why the issue of faith in the Old Testament was not a question of believing in the existence of God. The problem with people of that era was that they believed in far too many gods! We can sense the irony employed by the prophet Isaiah in describing our own efforts to anchor life through devotion to something less than God. He depicts the mechanics of constructing an idol. A workman puts a layer of gold over it or adorns it with silver chains. The carpenter chooses mulberry wood that resists rot to make sure it doesn't topple over. These creatures of our making are insignificant indeed before the One who stretched out the heavens like a curtain and who brings the princes and rulers to nothing. The power of the Lord does not pass away. Those who link their lives to God are able to "run and not be weary" and "walk and not faint" (Isaiah 40:31).

The question of God, and knowing God, is not first a question of existence at all. Rather, it is one about the nature of the Reality that envelops our lives, the Source that ushers us into life without our bidding, and the Destiny that receives us when we have

---

9   This discussion draws upon and is indebted to H. Richard Niebuhr's essay "Faith in Gods and in God," in his *Radical Monotheism and Western Culture* (New York: Harper & Brothers, 1960), 114–26.

breathed our last. Dinah had the question right when she asked, "What shall we do if God is not our friend?"

The truth is that everyone, whether believing in God or not, faces a Last Reality, a final state of affairs over which we have no final control. In our brief lifetimes we witness the rising and falling of the generations and we know or read of the ascending powers and their demise. We stand at the gravesides of those we love. We witness the defeat of our causes and the withering of our powers. In short, people live before some Last Reality with which they must reckon. Some may curse that reality and call it fate, the way things are, or just reality. By whatever name it is called, that reality is there. The question is not whether it exists but how that reality is related to us. "What shall we do if God is not our friend?"

Obstacles to Faith

If the quest for God in its variety of expressions is a universal concern, then why are we not all believers? Why is it that growing numbers, particularly young adults, refer to themselves as "spiritual but not religious"? We sometimes think that the ebbing faith of our time is new, but a moment's reflection will prove that every epoch has its own challenges to faith. We began this chapter with Psalm 42, in which the quest for God is compared to the quest of thirsty deer. The writer of that psalm no sooner states this universal need than he confesses that the desperate thirst for God is not satisfied. The nights are accompanied by tears, and the days are filled with the taunting question: "Where is your God?" (v. 3). This confessional psalm contrasts the memories of close connection with God with the bleakness of living without God. The writer remembers Temple observances in the company of friends, singing praises and making thanksgiving to God. Now that season of joy and exultation is past, and the soul is disquieted. Our confessor testifies to life that is threatened with chaos. "Deep calls to deep / at the thunder of your cataracts; / all your waves and your billows / have gone over me" (v. 7). With this reference to the thundering waters, the poet reminds us that at creation God subdued the chaotic depths and separated the sea from the dry land. Now the poet feels the full force of the sea depths, and they threaten to overwhelm him.

The clash between remembered devotion and present despair daunts the psalmist. He is almost ready to succumb and feels forgotten by God. Yet in despair, our witness retains hope. "Hope in God; for I shall again praise him, / my help and my God" (v. 11).

Perhaps many of us have experienced at least a measure of this despair. And, one hopes, we, like the author, have held on to our hope in God. This psalm should remind us once again that our walk with God is not a fixed possession. A young man interviewed on radio told of his former activity in his church. He reported how much those associations meant to him. But then he said in despair, "I've done every job in that church, but I still haven't met Jesus." We may hope that he, like the psalmist, kept his hope in God, so once again he could experience God's divine help.

If we acknowledge the tenuous nature of faith, we have to ask ourselves what this means for connecting our fleeting lives to God. Our faith assures us that God is not limited by our limited vision. If the clouds on an overcast night obscure our view of the moon and the stars, this does not mean that the heavenly bodies have fallen from the sky. The problem is our atmosphere and not the stars. The poet of Psalm 42 is still a believer. He cries out to God because of his need. Even in God's seeming absence, God is here. "Hope in God; for I shall again praise him, my help and my God."

Practical Atheism

A billboard on an expressway in the Midwest a few years ago displayed this "letter" from God: "Loved your wedding. Why don't you invite me to your marriage? Signed, God." The writers of this and other similar ads call attention to practical atheism, the stance of living life, not in denial of God, but in obliviousness to God's presence.

This obstacle to genuine faith was also familiar to the writers of Psalms. They did not engage in debating God's existence, for that was not even a question in their minds. Their ire was directed at those who lived, not in denial of God's existence, but in a nonchalant disregard of God's claim on their lives. Psalm 14 (paralleled in Psalm 53) refers to unbelievers as individuals who are traveling on the wrong track and doing "abominable deeds" (v. 1), not merely as people who have reached an invalid conclusion about God. "Fools say in their hearts, 'There is no God'" (53:1). Some scholars suggest that this can also be translated, "God is not here."[10] Those dismissed as fools are the ones who *say in their hearts*—in their private deliberations—there is no God. This form of denial is not theoretical atheism but a pattern that utterly ignores God as the author of life.

———————————

10 Edwin McNeil Poteat, "Exposition Psalms 42–89," in *The Interpreter's Bible*, ed. George A. Buttrick (Nashville: Abingdon Press, 1955), 4:278.

Some years ago, a woman who was then in her thirties was visited by representatives of a theological seminary. She was known in her youth to have been an active member of a congregation whose beloved pastor had graduated from that seminary. She and her husband were very successful in the entertainment industry and very well compensated for their talent. Their annual income was reported to be in the vicinity of $20 million. The seminary representatives spoke with her about her former pastor and the congregation of which they were a part. They invited her to consider establishing a scholarship that would aid future students who were studying in preparation for Christian ministry.

The woman was obviously unmoved by the appeal. She reported that in her youth she had indeed been an active member of the congregation served by the seminary graduate, and she still appreciated him and his ministry. She said that she went to church in her youth because she liked to sing in the choir. Then, she continued, when she went to college, she stayed away from church because she liked to sleep in. One of her visitors suggested that most people sense the need to anchor their lives in something deeper than their own wishes. A full life, he suggested, is one founded in a faith that guides us through difficult times and sets our sights on goals in life that matter.

The woman listened and nodded at the observation but then responded, "I am sure that this is true for some people. I really don't feel that need myself. I suppose I would feel differently if something should happen to my husband or my six-year-old. But at the moment I don't feel the need for religious faith." As you might guess, there was no scholarship fund initiated that day!

The practical atheist is one who thinks and acts as if God is not here. Seldom is it expressed in such explicit fashion. Note once more that in Psalm 14, the "fool" who says there is no God is not faulted for some intellectual or theoretical failing. It is his action, not his thinking, that is at the base of his folly. Fools who deny God are corrupt and do "abominable deeds" (v. 1). They consume others as if they were commodities at their disposal. They act as if there are no ethical standards to which they are accountable. They do not deny that God is; they simply act as if God has no jurisdiction, no sway, over their lives.

One commentator remarks that the fools who are dismissed in Psalm 14 are essentially the very people we admire in our culture. They are self-assured, self-directed, and autonomous people. It is clear that they do not suffer internal conflicts about how their actions might affect the lives of others.[11] A moment's reflection will assure us that this spirit is alive and well today. We read regularly of the wealth of the top 1 percent growing exponentially while 25 percent of the children in not a few neighborhoods live in poverty. Movements to institute policies that would make a livable wage mandatory are vigorously resisted. Some of the most powerful believe that a society of vast and growing disparities can long endure. That, to repeat, is not theoretical atheism. It is a practical conclusion and reflects a working assumption that the justice of the Almighty does not matter and need not be a concern. "Have they no knowledge, all the evildoers / who eat up my people as they eat bread, / and do not call upon the LORD?" (v. 4).

---

11   J. Clinton McCann Jr., "Introduction, Commentary and Reflections on the Book of Psalms," in *The New Interpreter's Bible* (Nashville: Abingdon Press, 1996), 4:731.

Optional God?

The question of knowing God, the question of faith, is often put as if a world with God or without God is an option. Some assume that the world is complete in itself. For them the question of faith is whether we will posit God as a value-added accessory or add-on to a world that creates its own sense.

If faith is trust in and reliance upon a person, agent, thing, or activity, then it is clear that everyone has faith. Anyone who finds meaning or significance in life relies on some person, thing, cause, or activity to assure that meaning. The issue is not whether one has faith but rather how comprehensive an individual's faith is to be. Is one's faith found in belongings, friends and family, or causes? Or does it center on the God who is relied upon as the Source of the good gifts and the One utterly to be trusted?

> **The issue is not whether we have faith but rather how comprehensive our faith is.**

We are inaccurate when we refer to individuals as people with or without faith. The position of atheism is not a default or neutral position. Insofar as it represents a construction about what the world is like, and a commitment to act accordingly, atheism represents not a denial of faith but an alternative faith. Neither faith in God nor atheism can be proved in the way that we can prove that water boils at 212 degrees Fahrenheit. An atheist holds that the world is self-explanatory and needs no explanation. To a person of this conviction, moral standards have no transcendent status but are purely matters of human preference and choice. Those holding this view may be individuals of deep conviction who engage in heroic efforts to combat cruel and unjust actions against others. Their struggle for justice, however, may betray a faith deeper than their declarations. If the moral values they cherish and uphold are solely human choices and preferences, on what basis may they insist that others should be held accountable to them?

Each generation faces the issue of faith within the context of that generation's assumptions and conventional wisdom. Some eras are more hospitable to faith than others. The so-called modern conventional wisdom poses its own challenges to faith. We generally speak of the "modern" world as the period of the last three hundred years or so. This loose designation began with the radical doubt of a mathematician and philosopher named René Descartes (1596–1650). Descartes, disillusioned with the strife and discord created by disputes and wars over religion, set out to found his system of thought on indisputable facts. He began by doubting everything that it was possible to doubt. The one reality, he suggested, that he could not doubt was the reality of his own thought. "I think; therefore I am." On the basis of this unshakable reality, he built his philosophy.

The individualistic program of radical doubt coincided with the rise of modern scientific method. Instead of understanding the world in terms of general principles, the scientific method as outlined by Francis Bacon (1561–1626) employed the senses to weigh, measure, and dissect the world as it was. The amazing success of the empirical sciences led some to believe that we know only what we can observe and measure. Convictions that cannot thus be measured and weighed are merely personal. We can respect them as individual expressions or emotions, but they do not serve as a reliable foundation for knowledge of and in the real world.

The inheritance of the modern world, then, becomes a two-track route to knowledge, one based on facts and another on opinion. Since God, who by definition is the Source and Creator of all that is, cannot be measured and dissected as a specimen in the lab, the whole notion of a God has become problematic. For many, the everyday world is strictly the realm of what may be observed or seen. The category of "the divine" has become questionable, and this worldview that influences the way we view our knowledge of God can be summarized this way:

1. Distrust of traditional belief and a corresponding reliance on observable evidence
2. Reliance on individual experience instead of reference to communities of belief
3. Reduction of realities to their constituent parts (as in science) and explanation from those elements to the whole, rather than understanding realities holistically
4. Treatment of the world as a closed and deterministic system, thinking of the world as a machine rather than as a living organism
5. Confidence in increasing scientific knowledge as the sole means of progress for the human race

For those of this mind-set, the notion of God is transformed from an explanation of how the world came to be into a debatable and, to some, unnecessary addition to the known and observable world. In the minds of some, the realm of science and the realm of religious belief are not only separate realms but adversaries. Writers refer to the "warfare" of science against religion. Charles Darwin's *Origin of the Species* (1859) outlined the concept of evolution in the delineation of the species. Some of his most ardent supporters have argued that the theory of the evolving species and the mutations from randomly acquired characteristics provided an adequate explanation of the natural world. For them the notion of a world that is purely random and purposeless renders God unnecessary.

In view of the success of science in explaining the physical world, for some, science also became a sole and sufficient explanation for the full range of human experience. This "scientism," which became an adversary of religious belief, was not itself a scientific conclusion. Rather, it represented a worldview of those who based their conviction on an exaggerated estimate of the range and capacities of science.

Atheism, the denial of the existence of God, rose as an available option for some who were devoted to "scientism." In the nineteenth century, some who denied the existence of God sought explanations for the fact that many people believed in God. Since their beginning assumption was that there was no God, they concluded that some explanation must be necessary. Ludwig Feuerbach (1804–1872) explained God as a human creation, a projection of an imaginary figure created by humans themselves. Sigmund Freud (1856–1939) held that belief in God was based on psychological forces deep within the psyche. And Karl Marx (1818–1883) held that religious belief in God was founded on economic forces and served as an opiate to those ravaged by those market forces. Since all three of these theorists assumed atheism as a beginning point, it is not surprising that they found it necessary to propose explanations for the continuing religious impulse of men and women in their day. Their view, and the view of many who followed, was that "God" was introduced only to explain what science had not yet been able to explain. Some held that as science gave convincing and adequate answers to further unsolved mysteries, the notion of God would become less and less compelling to serious-minded people and that religious belief would eventually fade and disappear. This was later referred to as the "God of the gaps."

Since science is a primary driver of the contemporary mindset, it is unfortunately true that some in religion and science have come to regard the two as inevitable foes. Some devotees of science believe that their field of study and research is able to give a full explanation of what is knowable and view religion as an individual opinion that has no legitimate claim for representing a real world of facts. On the other hand, some people in religion offer the view that religious belief and revealed truths are the ultimate arbiter of truth and that those truths are to be honored whenever they contradict the findings of science. Thus, the first chapters of Genesis are taken not only as affirmations of faith in God the Creator but also as scientifically correct descriptions of the process of creation. The conflicts between these camps continue in well-publicized form to this day.

But these positions representing the warfare of science and religion do not represent the total situation. Sizable numbers of people in both communities recognize that science and religion represent different forms of knowing and that they relate to different realms of reality, utilize different methods, and aim at different results. Science can describe the way the natural world works. Religion, on the other hand, explores the wider questions of its purpose and background. Why is there anything at all? Why is there a world? Is the world congenial to human purposes, or indifferent? These questions are beyond the scope of science.

Those who believe in God believe that this world has its source and purpose in God. Therefore, they are convinced that while science and religion constitute different realms of knowing, what is known by science cannot ultimately conflict with what is known by faith, since God is the object of both. Therefore, they see science and theology as complementary efforts to gain the truth, as much as limited human minds can comprehend it.

The Postmodern World and Science

For some time there have been challenges to the modern mind-set. As early as the late 1930s, Arnold Toynbee coined the term *postmodern* to describe an outlook that followed the perspective of the modern mind-set, or *modernity*. The term refers to a changed outlook in a variety of human activities. Art in the post-modern perspective can center more in the artist's consciousness than on a world outside the artist that was depicted in the painting or sculpture. In literature the writers can feel free to abandon the story line and concentrate instead on the inner thoughts of the author.

There has been a general perception that our ways of thinking and acting need to undergo significant change. In the 1970s, Willis Harman, then associated with the Stanford Research Institute, wrote that the challenges to an industrial civilization could not be corrected through modest changes. It is not, he suggested, that we are failing to live up to our values relating to the economy, war, poverty, and the environment. The problem, rather, is that our values themselves are counter to our survival. The need, he said, is for changes so basic and so comprehensive that they can be compared to the Greek word *metanoia*, a basic transformation of mind. He did not note, however, that this term is also used in the New Testament to refer to repentance and conversion.

What is the shape of the basic changes that are taking place from the postmodern perspective?

1. One decided change is in the role of the individual. The presumption was that each person deciphers and interprets the world as an individual. The postmodern perspective is that we understand the world as members of a culture, a society, and a community, not as solitary observers. Systems of meaning by which we understand the world take shape and are reinforced by communities. Those communities help shape and validate basic ways of looking at the world and understanding our role in it.

2. Consistent with the emphasis on community, the postmodern perspective points to the role of language in our understanding of the world. We encounter the world with the assistance of language. It helps select what we actually see and how we understand what we perceive. Indeed, some researchers argue there is growing evidence that we may not be able to see something until we have a way of describing it. For example, the Himba people in Namibia have no single word for the color blue. One word in their language refers to dark shades of blue, red, green, and purple. With this in mind, it is understandable that when members of the community were shown a circle consisting

of eleven green squares and one blue square, they had great difficulty in differentiating the blue square from the green squares that encircled it.[12]

3. The postmodern perspective particularly insists that we cannot claim to see the world from an absolute standpoint. We see it from a definite location in history, in culture, and in geography. That location, as well as the language we use, helps shape what we can see and how we see it. According to this conviction, we cannot see the world from a so-called objective point of view. We see it through the lenses made available by our location.

4. What we see is viewed not only through our social location but through the theories that we bring to the world. We see the world not as the world is but as we are. Einstein said, "Whether we can observe a thing or not depends on the theory which you use. It is the theory which determines what can be observed."[13]

5. The conclusions we reach concerning the world are not "proofs," but rather they represent the best explanations of which we are capable. Formerly, there were certain foundational convictions that were unchallenged and

---

12 Ellie Zolfagharifard, "Could Our Ancestors See Blue?" *DailyMail.Com,* March 2, 2015, http://www.dailymail.co.uk./sciencetech/article-2976405/Could -ancestors-blue-Ancient-civilisations-didn-t-perceive-colour-didn-t-word -say-scientists.html.

13 Comment made in 1925 in conversations with physicist Werner Heisenberg. See Werner Heisenberg, *Der Teil und das Ganze* (Munich: R. Piper, 1969), 49. Referred to also in Abdus Salam, *Unification of Fundamental Forces: The First of the 1988 Dirac Memorial Lectures* (Cambridge University Press, 1990), 99.

unchallengeable. Arguments for our view of the world could be built on them as proof of our basic beliefs. Now it is recognized that any basic conviction can be challenged. The truth that we seek must be tested by whether it fits coherently or fails to fit with a larger picture that can be tested. However, at the deepest level no worldview, according to this perspective, can be objectively proven, because nothing is purely objective.

These changes in perspective represent serious challenges to the dominant modern perspective and potentially change our outlook on how God may be known. They place the matter of knowing God in a perspective different from the one that has been dominant in history for the last three centuries or so. A second major change has also taken place in the way science understands the world. As we saw, the advent of science played a role in raising questions about our knowledge of God and the world. Now the way that science understands itself has significantly changed, and those changes also put the manner of knowing God in a new perspective.

The primary picture of the world we have come to expect from science is modeled on a machine or, now more recently, a computer. In fact, the primary model for talking about the world in classical physics was the watch. It worked mechanically, and its operation was completely determined by the watchmaker. The world was composed of objects (atoms) that interacted with one another. In much of modern science, the assumption was that if we knew all the causes that were acting within our world, we could tell with precision what would happen in the future. For many who believed in God, they believed that God was like the unseen clock-maker who fashioned the system to work predictably and flaw-lessly, and from afar.

In the last century that picture of the world changed dramatically. Physicists concluded that, while laws formulated by Newton apply to general conditions, they break down in the study of sub-atomic physics. Instead of thinking of atoms as indivisible components of matter, we learn from particle physicists that the atom is made up primarily of empty space. According to Harvard particle physicist Lisa Randall, "The nucleus [of the atom] is as small compared to the radius of the atom as the radius of the Sun is when compared to the size of the solar system."[14] Many physicists hold to the theory of subatomic quarks, particles that many believe in but have never seen. They contend that these quarks are bound together to form protons or neutrons by the four fundamental forces: electromagnetism, gravity, the strong nuclear force, and the weak nuclear force. Some physicists believe that a basic building block for understanding matter involves extremely small vibrating strings; although investigation of those strings, according to Randall, is beyond the scope of any experiment that can be conceived. And according to the uncertainty principle of Werner Heisenberg (in 1926), we cannot measure both the position and the movement of subatomic particles. We can only know the probability of their location.

---

14 Lisa Randall, *Knocking on Heaven's Door: How Physics and Scientific Thinking Illuminate the Universe and the Modern World,* repr. ed. (New York: Ecco, 2012), 78–79.

New Perspectives on Faith

For those of us who are not physicists, the net effect of science is to make it clear that the world can no longer be simply divided into fact and faith. Both in religion and in science, what we can know is built on realities that we cannot prove. Massachusetts Institute of Technology astrophysicist Alan Lightman writes of the "crisis of faith" in his science, because "to explain what we see in the world and in our mental deductions, we must believe what we cannot prove."[15] This is not to suggest that religion and science are the same. They are two different ways of knowing the reality of the world, and each of the two follows a way of knowing that is appropriate to the reality it is seeking to under-stand. What is common to both, however, is that anything we can know that matters to us depends on assumptions (or faith) that we cannot prove.

The discussions that follow will outline the way faith is shaped and how it operates in the lives of individuals. Along the way, we will attempt to show that religious faith and science complement each other in knowing God and are not, as some have expressed, at war with each other.

Our aim will not be to *prove* that the perspective of Christian faith is true. Rather, we will attempt to show that the perspective of faith provides a deeper way of seeing and understanding what we experience in the world, which results in fulfilling and abundant

---

15 Alan Lightman, "The Accidental Universe: Science's Crisis of Faith," *Harper's* magazine, December 2011, 40, http://harpers.org/archive/2011/12/the -accidental-universe/.

living. We turn first to the place of the believing man or woman and consider the miraculous nature of faith itself.

REFLECTION QUESTIONS

1. As you observe your community and your own life, what is most important to people? Could any of them be termed *objects of devotion*? How would you evaluate them in the light of Martin Luther's statement that our gods are whatever we cling to and rely on? What or who reigns supreme in your life, in your family's life, in your church's life, and in your community's life?

2. What questions would you like to address to the woman who said that as long as her family was healthy, she had no need for religious faith?

3. If you had a mission statement for your life, what would you want to include? Share three things you want to accomplish in your lifetime.

4. How does identifying God as "what lasts when everything else is gone" affect your view of God? What might it mean that God is our friend? How might that influence how we live and how we act toward others?

5. How do you respond to the idea that atheists and believers alike have faith? Can the atheist's view of the world be proved? Can the nature of God be proved?

6. Share a time when your faith became real in your life.

7. Which do you believe is the greater obstacle today, practical atheism or outright disavowal of belief? Why?

8. Can you identify aspects of postmodernist points of view that you observe or encounter in your own experience? How does your outlook on the world influence what you observe and see in it? Share a time when you and another person had the same experience but saw different things or understood it differently.

The Mystery of Faith

When I look at your heavens, the work of your fingers, . . .
what are human beings that you are mindful of them?
—Psalm 8:3-4

Three Seconds before Midnight

Whenever we give it a moment's notice, we should be stunned by how tenuous is our stay on the planet and how recently we arrived. We can get a notion about how recently humans arrived when we reduce the 4.5 billion years of Earth's existence to a twenty-four-hour day. If our home planet was formed at 12:01 a.m., rudimentary forms of life, such as bacteria, begin appearing at 3:30 a.m. and continue to develop throughout the day. Then at 9:00 p.m. marine invertebrates begin to appear. Later, dinosaurs roam the earth, but they disappear at 11:40 p.m. Ancestors of chimpanzees and humans appear when one minute and seventeen seconds are left in the day. Modern humans arrive three seconds before 12:00 a.m.,[1] and a person born in the 1970s represents about one-thousandth of a second before the clock strikes midnight.

So it is fair to say that our stay on the time scale of the planet is less than a blink of the eye. It is further sobering to remember that our solar system itself came to birth more than 9 billion years after the universe was formed and that our sun is about halfway through its projected life span of 10 billion years. All around the vast universe new stars are forming, and other stars are collapsing into their deaths.

The writer of Psalm 8 did not have the benefit of a twenty-first-century consensus on the formation of the universe, but it took only a look at the nighttime sky for this writer to comprehend our status as very recent arrivals on this planetary home—three seconds before midnight. Contemplating the moon and the stars, the work of God's fingers, the psalmist wonders why the Sovereign of the universe should give us any attention: "What are human beings that you are mindful of them?" In the Jerusalem Bible, the verse is translated, "Ah, what is man that you should spare a thought for him, the son of man that you should care for him?" Ancient sages and contemporary astrophysicists agree on the relative insignificance of us humans in the grand scale of space and time.

> **If we are so insignificant in the grand scheme, why does God care for us?**

---

1 Francis S. Collins, *The Language of God: A Scientist Presents Evidence for Belief* (New York: Free Press, 2006), 148–49.

Yet the writer of the psalm does not let the matter rest with an expression of human insignificance. No sooner than our poet has wondered why God would give any heed to mere humans we hear the breathtaking affirmation that we are made "a little lower than God" and given dominion over God's vast creation. God has even crowned humans with glory and honor, terms usually reserved for royalty. And the psalm ends, as it began, with an affirmation of praise, "O LORD, our Sovereign, / how majestic is your name in all the earth!" (vv. 5-6, 9).

We should not quickly pass over the mystery reflected in this brief psalm. Here we are—latecomers to the party, constructed from carbon and heavier elements that are fused and forged in the stars, then expelled into space when they flamed out and died. Now God names us as stewards in charge of the universe and gives us a status only a little lower than God. How is it that we, breathed to life by the Creator, came to consciousness, then expanded our fleeting moments on Earth to imagine eternity and sing praise to our Divine Source?

What Are Mortals?

We start with the psalmist's impulse to recognize the insignificance of human beings before the specter of the evening sky. This is as it should be. Proper knowledge of God begins in sheer awe and wonder at the immensity of the power by which we came to be. When I served in a theological seminary, we invited the curator of a well-known planetarium to present a video on the known universe to our students and faculty. Theology students can easily be tempted to think that theological theories they encounter in their reading and lectures encapsulate and contain God, and they tend to forget, as one professor expressed, "we humans are at the mercy of the One we seek to understand."[2] The first step in thinking of God, it seemed to our seminary, is a vivid sense of mystery and a sense of the unimaginable power and love of God. A guided tour through the universe reminds us of our relative size and standing before the enormity and intricacy of creation.

The astronomer's screen presentation reminded us that our home is in the Milky Way galaxy, a gathering of more than 100 billion stars, one of them being our sun. If we boarded a jet and wished to travel to the next nearest star in the Milky Way neighborhood, traveling at 500 miles per hour, it would take us 5 million years to arrive. That is the closest star, next to our sun, in *our* galaxy! We are reminded that light travels at 186,000 miles per second. Distances within the universe are measured by the span that light travels in one year. Using that as a scale, it takes 100,000 years for light to travel across the Milky Way, our neighborhood. There are more than 100 billion galaxies in the known universe, and they are separated from one another by about 2 million light-years. Astronomers tell us that if we were cosmic giants strolling among the galaxies, the galaxies would appear to us as "illuminated mansions scattered about the dark countryside of space."[3] Doctrines and creeds are important, as we all know, but trying to contain God in a few phrases is like trying to empty the ocean with

---

2   Wesley J. Wildman, professor of theology and ethics, Boston University School of Theology, from a seminary catalog.
3   Alan Lightman, "Our Place in the Universe: Face to Face with the Infinite," *Harper's* magazine, December 2012, 36.

a teaspoon. The psalm writer was right to wonder why the God who created the heavens and the earth should give any regard to mere humans.

We are now told that the creation of our universe took place in a blazing instant about 13.7 billion years ago. We learn from those who study these matters that the unimaginably compressed matter of the universe burst forth with incredible speed and that it is still expanding at a staggering rate. The rate for galaxies that are 100 million light-years away is estimated at 5.5 million miles per hour, and that speed increases as their distance from us increases, making those galaxies that are 300 light-years from us travel at an estimated 16.5 million miles per hour.[4] The universe is continuing to expand at an accelerating pace. New stars are forming out of clouds of gas. Old stars are collapsing in the form of supernova and casting the elements formed in their interiors into the outermost reaches of space.

While scientists *as scientists* cannot tell us *why* we were created, they can report, to a degree, *how* we were created. Carbon and other heavier elements are created by nuclear fusion of hydrogen, helium, and beryllium and expelled into space when these stars explode with a light 100 million times the strength of the sun. In this sense, according to their theories, we are all sons and daughters of the stars![5] All the carbon in our bodies, which is the building block for life, was produced in the furnaces of the stars.

---

4   Brian Greene, *The Fabric of the Cosmos: Space, Time, and the Texture of Reality* (New York: Alfred A. Knopf, 2004), 229.

5   Alister E. McGrath, *Surprised by Meaning: Science, Faith, and How We Make Sense of Things* (Louisville: Westminster John Knox Press, 2011), 66ff.

A Little Lower than God

With this reminder of our derivative nature and our origins, it is astounding to read the psalmist's affirmation of our standing and role:

> Yet you have made them a little lower than God,
>> and crowned them with glory and honor.
> You have given them dominion over the works of your
>> hands;
>> you have put all things under their feet,
> all sheep and oxen,
>> and also the beasts of the field,
> the birds of the air, and the fish of the sea,
>> whatever passes along the paths of the seas.
>
> O LORD, our Sovereign,
>> how majestic is your name in all the earth! (Psalm 8:5-9)

The poet begins with questioning why God, whose hand created the moon and the stars, would give any heed to us, much less care about us. The Bible and science are both quite clear that humans emerged out of the rudiments of creation. In Genesis 2:7, we are told that God formed the first human out of the dust of the ground, and that collection of dust sprang to life when God breathed the breath of life into the nostrils of what then became human.

Contemporary science adds commentary on the rootedness of humans in the created world. We noted earlier that the carbon in our bodies was formed billions of years ago in the furnace of the stars. In other ways, as well, our bodies are linked to the stars and galaxies that preceded us. The late Arthur Peacocke, scientist and theologian, detailed our emergence from the dust, showing how we are embedded in the created order. He wrote:

> We are remarkably and intimately related to those events in the galaxies that produce . . . the iron that makes our blood red and the hemoglobin of our bloodstream. Every atom of iron in our blood would not have been there had it not been produced in some galactic explosion billions of years ago and eventually condensed to form the iron in the crust of the earth, from which we have emerged.[6]

How, then, are we a "little less than God"?

The psalmist clearly understands our dominion over the creation, our responsibility for its care, as a sign of the glory and honor God confers on humans. Perhaps contemporary views of the world can help us to understand the glory and honor that is bestowed upon humankind in spite of the seeming insignificance of our individual lives in the vastness of time and space. The truth of the matter is that it is in humans, and in humans only, that the immense creation first comes to consciousness, as far as we know. Out of the elements fused in the stars—the dust of the earth, as Genesis puts it—comes a creature who does not merely act on instinct and self-preservation. The human whom God has crowned with glory and honor is aware of being a creature and reflects on the nature of the world in which that life was given. This child of the universe considers that he or she will one day die and reaches

---

6   Arthur R. Peacocke, "Theology and Science Today," in *Cosmos as Creation: Theology and Science in Consonance*, ed. Ted Peters (Nashville: Abingdon Press, 1989), 31–32.

out to understand the immensity of the creation out of which he or she comes.

If we step back for just a moment, we must acknowledge how extraordinary it is that a creature formed from the dust should become conscious. By what mysterious power do we leap from a collection of atoms into living beings who are aware of our being and who reflect on the meaning of the whole of which we are a fragmentary part? We are told that the human brain includes about 85 billion cells with up to 10,000 connections for each cell. The amount of information stored in the brain is about a trillion gigabytes, or about 75 billion 16-gigabyte iPads.[7] The most eminent scientists in brain research as yet have no answer as to how this elaborate mechanism, the human brain, produces consciousness. One of these researchers, Dr. H. Sebastian Seung, speaks frankly of the limitations of present neuroscience: "We've failed to answer simple questions," he said. "People want to know, 'What is consciousness?' And they think that neuroscience is up to understanding that. They want us to figure out schizophrenia and we can't even figure out why this neuron responds in one direction and not the other."[8]

This illustrates that though humans are constituted of bodies and brains that are a part of the physical order, they undergo subjective experiences that cannot be explained solely through the physical order. Neurologists can give a description of the physical processes that lead to our experience of love, or duty, or compassion, but none of those explanations suffice to explain

---

7   James Gorman, "All Circuits Are Busy," *New York Times*, May 26, 2014, https://www.nytimes.com/2014/05/27/science/all-circuits-are-busy.html?_r=0.
8   Ibid.

the subjective essence of those experiences.[9] It is clear to many researchers, therefore, that consciousness and thinking are "emergent" properties of the brain.

It is difficult to say when a brain becomes a mind. We know that the thinking mind of a human depends on the circuitry of the brain, but it develops new properties that cannot be reduced to that circuitry.[10] Astrophysicist Paul Davies notes the exquisite and complicated balances that are necessary for life and particularly marvels at the ability of the mind to comprehend aspects of the universe: "The universe has not only given rise to life, it's not only given rise to mind, it's given rise to thinking beings who can comprehend the universe. Through science and mathematics, we can, so to speak, glimpse the mind of God."[11] This reminds us that astronomer Johannes Kepler (1571–1630) and physicist Isaac Newton (1642–1727) had both described their work as "thinking God's thoughts after him."[12]

Albert Einstein is often quoted as saying that "the eternal mystery of the world is its comprehensibility."[13] Who is not struck by the fact that through mathematics developed by human beings, arriving as we have "three seconds before midnight" on the earth's

---

9   Thomas Nagel, "The Core of 'Mind and Cosmos,'" *New York Times,* August 18, 2013, https://opinionator.blogs.nytimes.com/2013/08/18/the-core-of-mind-and-cosmos/.

10 Michael S. Gazzaniga, *Who's in Charge? Free Will and the Science of the Brain* (New York: HarperCollins, 2011), 124.

11 Paul Davies, with Freeman Dyson, "The Human Legacy of a Great Mind and a Wise Man," in *Einstein's God: Conversations about Science and the Human Spirit,* ed. Krista Tippett (New York: Penguin Books, 2010), 35.

12 Peacocke, "Theology and Science Today," 34.

13 Walter Isaacson, *Einstein: His Life and Universe* (New York: Simon & Schuster, 2007), 462.

day, we should be able to understand the workings of the universe? For example, in the eighteenth century, astronomers observed movements in the planet Uranus that did not conform to the predictions made under Newton's theory of gravity. But they did not give up on Newton's theory. They thought it was too elegant to be abandoned. Two mathematicians, J. C. Adams in England and U. J. J. Leverrier in France, worked independently on the problem. It occurred to them that the apparently irregular movement of Uranus was caused by a planet beyond Uranus that had not been observed. Both mathematicians calculated where the previously unseen planet should be according to Newtonian theory. Observers in 1846 confirmed their prediction, and the planet Neptune was discovered.[14] How is it that the mind of a mere mortal can discern and anticipate the intricate workings of the universe of which he or she is a tiny and transient participant?

Even those who are not explicitly religious cannot help but be moved by the resonance between the mind of humans and the physical universe. Janna Levin, physicist and novelist, said in an interview that if she were to lean toward spiritual thinking, it would follow the question, "Why is it that there is this abstract mathematics that guides the universe? The universe is remarkable because we can understand it. . . . It's really, really astounding that these little creatures on this little planet that seem totally insignificant in the middle of nowhere can look back over the fourteen-billion-year history of the universe and understand so much."[15]

---

14 John Polkinghorne, *Quarks, Chaos & Christianity* (New York: Crossroad, 2005), 16.

15 Janna Levin, "The World Feels More Spacious," in Tippett, *Einstein's God*, 153.

The writer of Psalm 8 stood in amazement before the conviction that the Sovereign of the universe had crowned humans with glory and honor and had granted them dominion over the world that God had made. Our sense of wonder is further compounded when we consider that God has given humans minds that can think God's thoughts after him.

How Majestic Is Your Name

It is natural, therefore, that the hymn represented in Psalm 8 begins and ends with a doxology, with praise for the Creator of the universe. The writer was struck in "radical amazement," as Rabbi Abraham Joshua Heschel terms it, that the Sovereign who had wrought the moon and the stars still cared for the human creatures that were also the work of God's hand. Consideration of the moon and the stars moved the psalmist to reverence and praise. It is striking that many theorists, whether or not they believe in God as a personal being, nonetheless are moved to reverence and religious devotion by their studies of the natural universe. Perhaps no one has spoken of this in more convincing terms than Albert Einstein. He explained how he regarded himself as a religious man: "Try and penetrate with our limited means the secrets of nature and you will find that, behind all the discernible laws and connections, there remains something subtle, intangible and inexplicable. Veneration for this force beyond anything we can comprehend is my religion." He further explained his experience of religion:

The most beautiful emotion we can experience is the mysterious. It is the fundamental emotion that stands at the cradle of all true art and science. He to whom this emotion is stranger, who can no longer wonder and stand rapt in awe, is as good as dead, a snuffed out candle. To sense that beyond anything that can be experienced there is something that our minds cannot grasp, whose beauty and sublimity reaches us only indirectly: this is religiousness. In this sense, and in this sense only, I am a devoutly religious man.[16]

If such reverence and awe before the mystery of God are the beginnings of faith, mystery is not the last or the only word to be used to describe faith. In the hymnbook of the Hebrew Scriptures, the psalms, we find testimony of those who offer praise to God as the One known not merely in mystery. God is also the Knower who discerns our thoughts and knows a word even before it is on our tongues, the inescapable Presence who goes before us and behind (Psalm 139). In the New Testament we are told that God discloses Godself in human form as the Word made flesh. We discern in Christ the purposes of God to give us life in abundance. In Christian context we see how God is known most fully in God's appeal to us in Jesus Christ.

At this point in the discussion we simply recognize the mystery that God, in creating a universe far beyond our power to imagine, has created human beings who are given the gift of consciousness and imagination. It is in these creatures, spawned by materials fused in the stars, that the created order has come to consciousness and reaches out to utter praise and give reverence to the Source of all that is.

---

16 Isaacson, *Einstein*, 384–85, 387.

If God has created us a little less than God, it is no wonder that there is a quest for eternity placed in our hearts. We have been given an awareness of a time when we *were* not and a time when we will no longer *be* as we are. We reach out for permanence and sometimes try to fortify our fleeting lives with money or power or fame. In our more reflective moments, however, we recognize that all our trophies will finally tarnish and decay, but God lasts when all else is gone. And God has placed eternity in our hearts.

{ **God has placed eternity in our hearts.** }

I wonder if we can understand our praise and worship as expressions not only of a collection of individuals but of a representative body of all God's creation. Does that seem a bit of a stretch? We are a part of the creation that has become aware that this majestic world is the creation of a loving God. We join with this company of mortals in rendering our hearts' devotion to the One who alone is worthy of our final praise. But look around: we are bombarded with hundreds of appeals aimed at us, asking for our devotion and praise. It may be as simple as asking us to buy a brand of soap. They may be appeals for wealth and fame. They may be refined as loyalty to communities or nations. All these have their place. But in devotion before God we establish our final loyalty, the One to whom we give our hearts' devotion and praise.

{ **Devotion to God establishes our final loyalty.** }

I find it breathtaking that we represent the whole band of mortals who arrived at three seconds before midnight and now employ our voices to sing hymns to laud and honor the One who set us forth in being. And we who call ourselves by the name of Jesus Christ and proclaim him Lord testify that, in the fullness of time, the God who created us for fellowship and love made his appeal through the Word made flesh and dwelt among us. We confess along with those who have gone before us that Jesus Christ is God made visible. Saint Paul told the Corinthians that "God was in Christ, reconciling the world to himself" (2 Corinthians 5:19 NLT). "So if anyone is in Christ, there is a new creation: everything old has passed away; see, everything has become new!" (5:17 NRSV).

The same Jesus Christ who assured us that God sees the sparrow fall and that we are of much more value than the sparrows also displayed on the cross the crucified God, who pours out sacrificial love to reconcile and redeem. The One who created the heavens and the earth shows us in Jesus Christ that we are forgiven and cherished. In raising Jesus Christ from the dead, God created a new humanity. And anyone who is joined with Christ lives in a new world. "O LORD, our Sovereign, / how majestic is your name in all the earth!" (Psalm 8:1, 9).

The God and Father of Jesus Christ our Lord still works with creation and longs to bring that good creation to its fulfillment. Limited as we are, our minds and imaginations do not do well in grasping the immensity of God's love and power. Jesus taught us to see the infinite in the near at hand. He taught in parables, stories of daily life, to teach us how God works in our midst.

The Creature Sings Praise

This story stands in my mind as a parable of God's relationship with us. A couple welcomed their first child, a baby girl, into their home.

They were thrilled that she had arrived, and they loved her with all their parental love.

But they also noticed that their lifestyle changed with the arrival of this baby. Sleep was rationed for a time in small modules. There were never-ending chores to care for this child. Frequently they called their normal activities to a halt to quiet the baby's crying and to attend to her needs.

On one such occasion, when the mother was trying to feed, clean, and pacify the child all at once, her parents were also visiting. In the middle of this frenzy of caring, the woman's father said to her, "Someday this little girl will tell you she loves you." Many months later the young mother called her dad and said, "Today it happened." The baby, now a toddler, had learned to put together a few words, and she said, "Mommy, I love you." Any memory of interrupted sleep and dislocated schedules was erased from the mother's mind.

A few years later the little girl had learned more words, and she was joined by a baby brother. For Christmas their father suggested that they get together to write a poem to their mother as a gift. He asked them what words they might use to say thanks to their mother. And the daughter, along with her little brother, thought of good things she had done for them. Acting as scribe, the father composed their poem of thanks. The poem ended with the words of the young daughter, "and she really, really loves me." The offspring gave praise and thanks to the one who had given her birth.

So it is that we, arriving three seconds before midnight, look to the heavens and say, "O Lord, our Sovereign, how majestic is your name in all the earth." The creature sings praise.

REFLECTION QUESTIONS

1. Does it affect your view of human life when you consider that we as humans arrived on the earth only three seconds before midnight in the planetary day? In what ways?

2. How should contemporary men and women view the statement of Psalm 8 that humans are created "a little lower than God"? What are signs to which you might point to support or to question that view?

3. In what way(s) would you attempt to explain how organisms such as humans, created from elements fused in the stars, should come to consciousness and ponder their origins and destiny?

4. Why do you believe this answer so far has eluded the experts?

5. What is the difference between describing electric activity in brain circuitry, on the one hand, and undergoing the experience of thought, the recognition of beauty, and the sense of moral obligation?

6. What are the privileges and obligations involved in having been given "dominion" over God's creation?

7. How does it affect your understanding of worship if you consider it an act on behalf of all the creation?

The Inevitability of Faith

*Now faith is the assurance of things hoped for,
the conviction of things not seen.*

—Hebrews 11:1

A circuit-riding preacher who was visiting for the first time in a frontier community wanted to learn the views of people in the area on the question of infant baptism. He put the question to a farmer: "Do they believe in infant baptism in these parts?"

"Man," the farmer responded, "I not only believe in it; I've seen it done!"

The farmer illustrates the division we frequently make between fact and faith. We look upon what we take as fact as what can be known for sure. Matters of faith, on the other hand, seem indefinite, disputable, and uncertain. We can verify matters of fact for ourselves by weighing and measuring. On the other hand, matters of faith differ, so we think, by being private matters, incapable of being proved true or false.

The problem with this disposition is that we are tempted to think that only measurable, datable facts are real. Thus, all other judgments are questionable or suspect, and one person's opinion is as good as another. Is that your experience? With this mind-set, faith becomes a wary acceptance of dubious viewpoints by an act of the will. Belief in God, rather than an affirmation of the central reality in the world, becomes instead a well-hedged speculation about which we give our assent. Wilfred Cantwell Smith summarized the resulting affirmation in these terms: "Given the uncertainty as to whether there is a God or not, as a fact of modern life, I announce that my opinion is 'yes.' I judge God to be existent."[1]

There must be amusement in heavenly realms when we humans, arriving on a planet three seconds before midnight, render our considered judgment on the question of whether the Creator and Sustainer of it all really exists!

This separation between fact and faith often prompts us to contrast faith and science. Science, with all the benefits it makes available, seems to operate solely on facts. Faith, in contrast, may seem to rest on disputable and uncertain opinions. In this chapter we look at this supposed easy distinction between fact and faith. Our central contention is that faith, far from being an impediment in what we can know about the realities of the world around us, is instead an essential ingredient in anything we can know, whether through science or in religion.

The Shape of Faith

To spell out what we mean, we need first to suggest what we mean by the term *faith*. There are perhaps almost as many definitions of

---

1 Wilfred Cantwell Smith, *Believing: An Historical Perspective* (Oxford, UK: Oneworld, 1998), 44.

this term as there are for *love*. Faith can mean almost anything: an unsupported hunch about something, an assumption about a person or thing, or even the name of a religious organization. Here is how scientist and theologian Alister McGrath has defined faith: "Faith is basically the resolve to live our lives on the assumption that certain things are true and trustworthy, in the confident assurance that they are true and trustworthy, and that one day we will know with absolute certainty that they are true and trustworthy."[2] It is clear immediately that faith in this definition is not merely or primarily passive assent to a dubious proposition. It is not fanciful speculation lacking a basis in reality. It is an action word. It refers to the act of trusting and relying on a reality and a confident expectation that our experience one day will confirm the validity of that trust.

Scientific knowledge is often contrasted with religious knowledge by suggesting that people pursue science in an utterly dispassionate and objective manner. The truth is that scientific knowledge—indeed, any knowledge—includes selectivity and discernment. What the scientist selects to observe is chosen in part on the basis of his or her theory of what the world is like. Albert Einstein said "Whether you can observe a thing or not depends on the theory which you use. It is the theory which determines what can be observed."[3] In short, we see what our theories permit us to see, what counts as fact.

---

2   Alister McGrath, *Doubting: Growing Through the Uncertainties of Faith* (Downers Grove, IL: IVP Books, 2006), 27.

3   Comment made in 1925 to Werner Heisenberg and quoted in Salam, *Unification of Fundamental Forces* (see chap. 1, n. 13).

Many will be familiar with experiments in which people with different backgrounds view a video. When observers are asked about what they saw, they generally give widely varying accounts. Viewing the same video, they nonetheless see different things. Some notice the colors and clothing styles worn by the actors. Another remembers their hairstyles. Each of the viewers selects features of the video in keeping with his or her history, gender, wishes, hopes, and stereotypes. It has been said that we do not see the world as it is; we see the world as we are. Our notion of the dispassionate objectivity that underlies some of our knowledge fails to acknowledge what we contribute to selecting and interpreting our experience.

We should also recognize that scientific knowing assigns values to certain kinds of answers and not others. Science is not value-free. Researchers favor solutions to problems that are elegant, beautiful, and simple. There is an implicit faith that nature itself favors those qualities. We referred in chapter 2 to Albert Einstein's reference to the feeling elicited by mystery as the basis for all art and science. It is clear that Einstein the scientist saw the world through the lenses of something like a faith, even if that faith was not in a personal God. In fact, any study of the natural order takes place in the context of the faith that the universe is rational, orderly, and dependable. Thomas Huxley, an enthusiastic interpreter of the work of Charles Darwin, held that science and religion should not be interwoven. He was critical of interference by the church in scientific discussions. But this did not mean, in his mind, that science was bereft of its own form of faith. In 1885 Huxley spoke at the dedication of a statue to Darwin. Despite Huxley's desire to separate religion and science, he insisted that science operated out of faith: "The one act of faith in the convert to science . . . is the confession of the universality of order and of the absolute validity in all times and under all circumstances, of the law of causation," he said. "This confession is an act of faith, because, by the nature of the case, the truth of such propositions is not susceptible of proof."[4]

In emphasizing that faith is involved in all forms of knowing, and not just as an element in religious knowing, we should stress that the "faith" to which we refer may be faith in a purposeless universe, not necessarily a universe that reflects design, purpose, and intelligence. Science and theology are increasingly addressing some of the same questions. Science reporter James Gleick even claims that "God's turf" now belongs "not to the theologian but to the scientist."[5]

Alan Lightman, a physicist at Massachusetts Institute of Technology, writes of his faith in the accidental nature of the universe. He terms any evidence that seems to contradict that assumption as a "crisis of faith" for the scientist.[6]

To his credit, Lightman cites substantial evidence that would put in question his faith in the accidental universe. He refers, for example, to evidence for the "fine-tuning" of the universe, evidence for an apparent direction built into the universe to favor and provide for the creation of life. The "fine-tuning" argument

---

4   Charles Darwin, *The Life and Times of Charles Darwin* (1887), quoted in McGrath, *Surprised by Meaning*, 38 (see chap. 2, n. 5).

5   James Gleick, "Science on the Track of God," *New York Times Magazine*, January 4, 1987, 2, http://www.nytimes.com/1987/01/04/magazine/science-on -the-track-of-god.html.

6   Lightman, "The Accidental Universe," 35 (see chap. 1, n. 15).

cites a number of delicately balanced forces in the universe, the slightest variation in any one of which would have made life impossible. One of those exquisitely balanced forces is the nuclear force that binds elements together. If the nuclear force were stronger by the slightest measure, then hydrogen elements would fuse with other hydrogen atoms to make helium and eliminate all hydrogen in the universe. If there were no hydrogen, there could be no water, and hence, no life. On the other hand, if the nuclear force were weaker, then the complex atoms necessary for biology would not have held together, and there would be no life. The slightest variation in either direction would have made life impossible. This is only one of the many instances that illustrate an apparent purpose inherent in the universe toward the creation and sustenance of life. Lightman acknowledges that this constitutes strong evidence of purpose and for the existence of God. Yet he dismisses this natural conclusion with the comment that the existence of God "does not appeal to most scientists."[7] It is astonishing to hear an empirical scientist reject the strong evidence of his observations solely on the grounds that the identification of purpose in the universe clashes with his and others' personal preferences in the matter. Clearly his faith that the world is purposeless has won out over the impressive evidence that appears to lead to a different conclusion.

Lightman has a theory that he believes explains the appearance of purpose in the universe. He and others who share his view posit the existence of "countless" universes of which ours is only one. In their view our universe appears to be fine-tuned simply because it "happened" to be one of the billions of universes that are disposed

---

7   Ibid., 37.

to promote life. This accidental happening, in their view, is outweighed by countless other universes—universes that we have not observed and that in fact could not be observed—in which conditions are not oriented toward the creation of life. The multiuniverse theory is clearly an act of faith. Not one of these posited universes has been or could be observed. It is an elaborate creation proposed to lend credibility to a faith that the one universe we can observe is purely accidental and devoid of purpose and intent. To explain the advantages of the multiuniverse theory, Lightman approvingly cites the words of Nobel Prize–winning physicist Steven Weinberg: "Over many centuries science has weakened the hold of religion, not by disproving the existence of God but by invalidating arguments for God based on what we observe in the natural world. The multiuniverse idea offers an explanation of why we find ourselves in a universe favorable to life that does not rely on the benevolence of a creation, and so if correct will leave still less support for religion."[8]

Lightman concludes that the theory is difficult for many of his colleagues to embrace. It requires them, he says, not only to view the universe as accidental but to believe in the existence of many other universes, whose existence they cannot prove. "Thus, to explain what we see in the world and in our mental deductions, we must believe what we cannot prove." He terms this science's "crisis of faith." "Theologians are accustomed to taking some beliefs on faith," says Lightman. "Scientists are not."[9] We should add that his unflinching faith has not only required him to defy

---

8   Quoted in ibid., 38.
9   Ibid., 40.

considerable evidence of purpose in the known world but to posit a constellation of other universes for which there is no empirical evidence. This is a leap of faith that dwarfs the faith required to interpret the one universe we can observe as a realm of purpose and intent.

Another physicist, John Polkinghorne, insists that positing trillions of universes in order to avoid the appearance of purpose is unscientific. It is not science to propose multiple universes, says Polkinghorne, since we have no access to any universe other than our own. Polkinghorne terms the multiuniverse theory a "metaphysical guess." He suggests that it is much more "economical" to view this world not just as "any old world" but as a universe endowed with purpose by its Creator.[10]

Faith, Science, and the Search for Truth

Our discussion to this point shows that some form of faith is a significant element in anything that we can know, whether it is our scientific views of the world or our knowledge of God. We have held that the world cannot be divided neatly between matters of fact and matters of faith. Faith and theory are interwoven with what we observe on all the questions that are most important to us. Science and religion both employ unproved and unprovable assumptions about the world and its origins.

To be sure, religious faith and the elements of faith in scientific explanation are not the same. Religious faith is more

---

10 John Polkinghorne and Nicholas Beale, *Questions of Truth: Fifty-one Responses to Questions about God, Science, and Belief* (Louisville: Westminster John Knox Press, 2009), 13–14.

comprehensive in its reach than scientific learning. In seeking to know God, we are reaching for the most comprehensive interpretation of the universe and seeking to understand not only how the universe works, as in science, but what purposes and intentions are reflected in it. Indeed, religion asks the most fundamental question: Why is there anything? And we recognize that even our raising the question of purpose and intention is itself an act of faith.

In the chapter that follows we will look at the question of faith in knowing God. In this chapter, we are giving attention to elements of faith that are evident in all our knowing, whether religious or scientific. We take to heart the words of the distinguished geneticist Francis Collins, who headed the Human Genome Project: "The God of the Bible is also the God of the genome. He can be worshiped in the cathedral or the laboratory. His Creation is majestic, awesome, intricate and beautiful—and cannot be at war with itself. Only we imperfect humans can start such battles. And only we can end them."[11]

Personal Interest and Knowing

We should agree that some personal interest is involved in anything of significance we can know. We referred earlier in this chapter to the physicist who admitted that his faith in randomness and chance was threatened by evidences of purpose. He had an interest in demonstrating that the world does not reflect the presence of mind or purpose. Furthermore, scientific pursuits do not aim

---

11   Collins, *The Language of God*, 211 (see chap. 2, n. 1).

at arriving at just any workable resolution of a problem. Scientists seek answers and theories that are beautiful and elegant. There is a built-in assumption that scientific solutions that are simple and elegant are more likely to be true.

Knowledge of God likewise involves a strong personal interest. We are hardly indifferent and neutral on whether there is a God and what the disposition of that God is toward us. When we raise the question of God, we are concerned about the destiny and grounding of our lives. To be human is to live before the reality of the seeming nothingness of death. There will be a time when we no longer are. Furthermore, we know that not only we, but those we love, the accomplishments we achieve, the institutions and causes that we serve will one day perish and decay. This drives us to the question that we cited earlier from George Eliot's Dinah, who asked her congregation, "What shall we do if God is not our friend?"[12] What in a world that witnesses the passing of all that we prize can we look to and depend on? The question of knowing God, therefore, is a question bearing upon our deepest identity and selfhood.

Building a Worldview

To explore the world in any dimension, we operate with a view of what the world is like. Is it hostile or benign? Is it a place of universal order or chaos? All of us operate with certain, perhaps unspoken sentiments about what the world is like. That worldview requires forming a picture of the whole realm of reality of

---

12 See chapter 1.

which we are a minute and fleeting element. For this reason, it is misleading to suggest that our choice is to have faith or not to have faith. The real question, rather, is what kind of faith we will have. An atheist is not a person without faith. The atheist, like the believer, has some picture of the world that is incapable of being proved.

We observe that when a person stops believing in God he or she will often transfer faith and devotion from God to another object of faith. Some secular worldviews, for example, demand allegiance and assume qualities characteristic of religious movements. Certain of these, for example, imbue political movements or causes with religious qualities. Historians have noted that political movements share qualities with religion such as centering on an "ultimate concern, the building of a community, the appeals to a common narrative and symbols, and requiring certain behavior from its adherents."[13]

Occasionally, people who once lived in the light of some religious faith say that they have lost their faith. Perhaps it would be more accurate to say that they have *altered* their faith. One individual meeting this description announced that he no longer had faith. He took some risks in making this announcement, but he did it out of his conviction about the necessity of being honest. He could not bring himself to pretend and deceive others about what he believed and what he could no longer believe. Furthermore, he disclosed that he would find his solace and meaning in his family relationships and in pursuit of music and literature. Disagree

---

13 Alister McGrath, *Why God Won't Go Away* (Nashville: Thomas Nelson, 2010), 65ff.

though we do about his theological conclusions, we can admire his rigorous honesty and the value he found in family and art. But this was not a case of abandoned faith; it was a faith redirected. He was acting on a conviction, incapable of being proved, about the value of honesty, family, and art.

We recall that Martin Luther said that whatever we cling to and rely on is our god. In this perspective, then, it is clear that this individual was a believer, even if not a believer in God. We should note that one who has faith in God might no less prize honesty, family, and art. However, the one who has faith in God could well insist that the values of honesty and the love of family and art have their deepest meaning because they are a gift of God and grounded in God.

Knowledge and the Limits of Imagination

Whatever form our faith may take, we have to recognize that the reality in which we place our faith is not limited by the strength of our imaginations. Our imagination and reason are stretched beyond their capacity if we seek to encompass God in the confines of our mind. At times even the strongest believers are stunned to think of the claims that are made. What happens when we pray? If there are more than 100 billion stars in the Milky Way, our sun being one of them, and more than 100 billion other galaxies of similar size in the universe, how could God know us by name, hear our prayers, and sustain us in sorrow and joy? How is it possible that God could read the intent of our spirits and know a word before it is on our lips, as Psalm 139 assures us is the case? How can we imagine that in the vastness of the universe, we can cast all our anxiety upon God and be assured, in the words of 1 Peter 5:7, that God cares for us?

The fact that human imagination is incapable of fitting these truths of faith into a conventional rational pattern is not an indication that they are impossible or untrue. Jesus made claims about the redeeming love of God that in no way fit with the experience and imagination of his hearers. Perhaps this is why Jesus's characteristic method of teaching was in parables. In these parables Jesus made the case for the goodness and love of God, which is far beyond our comprehending in normal terms. Through his parables, we can more readily understand. We cannot grasp how God seeks out the lost and welcomes them with forgiving love, but we can relate to a father who risks losing face by going out on the road to meet a returning son who had repudiated and humiliated him. That is the face of redeeming love made vulnerable in order to restore a relationship. Jesus placed it in human terms that we can understand.

> The fact that human imagination is incapable of fitting truths of faith into a conventional rational pattern is not an indication that they are impossible or untrue.

We should note that religious faith is not alone in confronting the inevitable limits of human imagination. Niels Bohr, Nobel laureate for his research in subatomic physics, said, "If you are not completely confused by quantum mechanics, you do not understand it."[14] He either had to abandon his view of the world of classical

---

14 Niels Bohr, quoted in Lisa Randall, *Knocking on Heaven's Door: How Physics and Scientific Thinking Illuminate the Universe and the Modern World*, repr. ed. (New York: Ecco, 2012), 10

physics or "abandon his belief in observed reality."[15] He had to conclude that the laws of classical physics do not apply in the miniscule distances occupied by electrons in an atom.

The field of subatomic physics is a field of science, but it exceeds the imagination even of those who are schooled in it. Physicists studying the atom, as we have seen, describe the subatomic world as composed primarily of empty space within which there is a system not unlike our solar system.[16] The whole field of nanotechnology involves discussions of dimensions so small that our imaginations fail to comprehend them. Anyone reading the reports of quantum physics must be prepared to imagine how objects can be in two places at once, how light can be both a wave and a particle, and how one object can influence another when there is no obvious connection between the two ("entangled particles").[17] If we believe that the scientist simply reports on what is seen and measured, we may be taken aback when a particle physicist reports that he believes in quarks (inside the protons of the nucleus of an atom) but that he has never seen one and believes that no one ever will see them. They may defy imagination, but they "make sense of a lot of physical experience."[18]

These examples from the scientific world are not intended to compare with the questions that occur to the believer in knowing God, but they do illustrate that religious faith is not alone in locating realities that we can believe in and rely on, even if they exceed our capacity to imagine or comprehend. The limitation is in our

---

15   Randall, *Knocking on Heaven's Door*, 80.
16   Ibid., 78.
17   Greene, *The Fabric of the Cosmos*, 114 (see chap. 2, n. 4).
18   Polkinghorne, *Quarks*, 116 (see chap. 2, n. 14).

capacity to imagine and not in the divine mystery that we seek to know more fully.

Knowledge in the Absence of Proof

What is most important for us to know can seldom be proved. Neither the proposition that the world reflects the mind of God nor the view that the world is purposeless and chaotic is capable of definitive proof. We saw in the foregoing paragraphs that some sweeping theories about the nature of the world have never been proved and can never be proved. Yet they are believed and affirmed because they "make sense" of a whole sphere of experience.

We can take it as a fact of life that we cannot provide absolute proof on the basic questions of life. Matters of definition, such as two plus two equals four, can be proved within a mathematical system, but few would lay down their lives for that proposition. Whether or not it is raining outside can also be proved by stepping out the door, but our demonstrable answer to that question is hardly life-changing. However there are convictions that matter much to us. To affirm that God is love or that I know my friend is trustworthy or that it is blessed to be kind can never be proved. Yet these are convictions in which we can believe and for which we can risk and suffer. Tennyson said, "Nothing worth proving can be proven nor yet disproven."[19] We should not be surprised, and we should not be dissuaded from belief in God, simply because we

---

19 Alfred Lord Tennyson, "The Ancient Sage," in *The Oxford Book of English Mystical Verse*, ed. D. H. S. Nicholson and A. H. E. Lee (Oxford University Press, 1917).

are unable to prove God's existence. While no one has seen God, belief in God and the life of faith in God help us make sense of and live with hope and bearing in that world.

Knowledge, Faith, and Hope

Faith is closely allied with hope, as it is with love. In Paul's first letter to the church in Corinth, he holds that faith, hope, and love abide. And faith, incapable of proof, looks forward expectantly to the time when what we believe in faith will be certified in sight: "Now I know only in part; then I will know fully, even as I have been fully known" (1 Corinthians 13:12). The definition of faith cited earlier in this chapter referred to a commitment to act on the assumption that certain things are true, the confidence that they are in fact true, and the assurance that they will be fully disclosed to be true. There is a sense of incompletion with faith. In faith we live on the basis of what we cannot prove. But we look forward in hope to the full disclosure of what we now hold for true and depend on, praying with the hymn writer: "And, Lord, haste the day when my faith shall be sight, the clouds be rolled back as a scroll."[20]

This sense of completion, the longing for a fuller disclosure of what is now held in faith, is present in the implicit faith of science as well. Operating on the faith that the universe is ordered and rational, the work of scientific exploration is driven by the thirst to gain a greater grasp on the nature of that order. It is sustained in the confidence that informed research will lead

---

20 "It Is Well with My Soul," written by Horatio Spafford, 1873, in *The United Methodist Hymnal* (Nashville: United Methodist Publishing House, 1989), 377.

to fuller disclosures. John Polkinghorne, particle physicist and theologian, traces some of the efforts in the history of science to reach a more inclusive grasp of the fundamental forces in the universe. He confesses his own hopes for a "Grand Unified Theory" (GUT for short) that will relate the strong nuclear forces in nature, and perhaps gravity, the weakest of the four fundamental forces.

Some believe that the best candidate for that integrating theory is the so-called string theory, but this is an uncertain hope. Study of string theory focuses on details that are millions and millions of times smaller than anything that can be observed. Polkinghorne observes that "this act of faith by the physicists is a reflection of a trust, doubtless unconsciously entertained, in the consistency of the one God whose will is the origin of the order of the created universe."[21] Perhaps it is this consideration that moved Stephen Hawking, as we observed, to compare finding the grand unifying theory of the universe to knowing the mind of God.[22]

Conclusion

Our discussion in this chapter has led us to identify an element of faith in any search for truths on questions that are of significance to us. We have noted that elemental faith, often unexpressed or unacknowledged, is involved in science, as well as in theological studies. This has led us to contend that science and theology are

21 John Polkinghorne, *Quantum Physics and Theology: An Unexpected Kinship* (New Haven, CT: Yale University Press, 2007), 99.

22 Hawking, *A Brief History of Time*, 175 (see chap. 1, n. 6).

complementary ventures in searching for truth, even though they are sometimes viewed solely as adversaries. It is true, of course, that some scientists, including some to whom we have referred, deny any discernible purpose in the universe. We need to note, however, that such a stance is a matter of faith and not a product of scientific discovery. Science deals with *how* things happen and not *why* they happen. The existence of purpose in the world and the nature of its origins are not scientific questions but matters of personal belief. Science neither confirms religious faith nor disconfirms it.

In view of the element of faith that we have found to be involved in varying degrees with our diverse methods of searching for truth, we may identify some characteristics that are to be found to be present both in knowing God and in scientific research:

1. The search for truth is a matter reflecting personal passion and interest, not a dispassionate or solely objective undertaking.
2. Our investigations take place within a worldview or theory that is not itself capable of being proved.
3. Fidelity to what we experience may involve us in explanations or interpretations that are beyond our capacity to imagine.
4. Inclusive convictions about the reasons behind the world are matters of faith and as such cannot be proved or disproved.
5. Searches for the truth, whether in theology or in science, are spurred forward and sustained by faith that there is unifying truth to be found and that it will one day be revealed.

We have noted that the nature of science has meant that more and more scientists are now examining questions that formerly were the province of theology alone. Some have noted that even scientists who are agnostic are beginning to sound more and more like theologians. Robert Jastrow, an agnostic and an astrophysicist, exhibits self-deprecating humor in describing the present moment in the cooperative search for truth:

> At this moment it seems as though science will never be able to raise the curtain on the mystery of creation. For the scientist who has lived by his faith in the power of reason, the story ends like a bad dream. He has scaled the mountains of ignorance; he is about to conquer the highest peak; as he pulls himself over the final rock, he is greeted by a band of theologians who have been sitting there for centuries.[23]

REFLECTION QUESTIONS

1. Does it affect your view of faith significantly when it is defined as a resolve to act on a conviction rather than merely to agree to a proposition? Can you recall ways that faith has functioned for you in the former way? In the latter?

2. How do you think that the validity of faith understood as the resolve to act on a conviction is confirmed? How does

---

23 Robert Jastrow, *God and the Astronomers*, 2nd ed. (New York: W. W. Norton, 1992), 107.

that differ from the way you confirm a proposition? What insights about faith do you gain from your answer?

3. In what way can the view that the universe has no purpose and that there is no God be an example of faith? Can it be proved? What are the practical consequences of such a view?

4. Why do you think that scientific theories that are simple, elegant, and beautiful are considered more apt to be true than those that are not? What implications would you draw from conviction? What questions would you ask?

5. Have you known someone who has been said to have "lost" his or her faith? Can you identify objects of faith that are embraced in the absence of faith in God? In what ways is it appropriate to speak of this as an alteration, rather than a loss, of faith?

6. Is it credible to you to hold that there are certain things in science and in religious faith that are true that cannot be imagined? Is the realm of things that are true limited to those things we are capable of imagining?

Faith as Trust

*I am convinced that neither death, nor life, nor angels, nor rulers, nor
things present, nor things to come, nor powers, nor height, nor depth,
nor anything else in all creation, will be able to separate us from the
love of God in Christ Jesus our Lord.*

—Romans 8:38-39

The discussion in the last chapter contended that some measure of
faith is required in order to know anything that really matters to us.
Our choice is not between faith and fact. As one has put it, "We
do not come to know anything except by believing in something."[1]
Faith is intermixed in anything we can know. In this chapter we
turn to faith as a means of knowing God and seek that form of
faith which is most appropriate to knowing God.

When we speak of faith in God, we are speaking primarily of
faith as trust in and commitment to God. The word for "faith"
in the New Testament Greek, *pistis*, and its corresponding verb,

---

1   Lesslie Newbigin, *Truth and Authority in Modernity* (Valley Forge, PA: Trinity
Press International, 1996), 3.

pisteuo, most frequently refer to the act of trusting or the trust-worthiness of the object of faith. It can also denote the contents of what is believed. The New Testament does not use "faith," as we sometimes do in casual conversation, to refer to an opinion that is held without proof.

The Meaning of Faith

As we read the New Testament in English, we sometimes forget that "faith" typically refers to an active commitment of the whole self and not merely to assent to an opinion unsupported by the evidence. The process of translation has not always served us well in keeping this understanding before us. When the New Testament was translated into Latin, *pisteuo* was translated into *credo*, which was based on *cor do,* which means "I give my heart." Since we have no action word in English for "faith," these words, *pisteuo* and *credo*, were in turn translated into our English Bible as "belief." "Belief" was derived from the German word *belieben,* meaning "to love."[2] The problem posed for our English New Testament is that the word *belief* has undergone significant changes in the past two or three centuries. It often now signifies assent to a proposition that is perhaps uncertain or dubious.

With this history in mind, we need to remind ourselves that the faith involved in knowing God is not just nodding assent to a proposition about the reality referred to as "God." Faith is active trust and commitment. Its object is not primarily a proposition; rather, it refers to a relationship of trust to another subject, agent

---

2   Karen Armstrong, *The Case for God* (New York: Alfred A. Knopf, 2009), 87.

or, in this case, God. In the words used in our definition in chapter 3, faith is a "resolve to live our lives on the assumption that certain things are true and trustworthy." Faith is an action of the whole thinking, willing, feeling self reaching out in relationship to the final Reality of the universe, to God, in trust and reliance as Source and Sustainer of our lives and our soul's true good.

Perhaps the best analogy or parable of the faith involved in our relationship to God is the language traditionally used in the covenant of Christian marriage. Faith, we have said, refers not primarily to assent but to a relationship. In the covenant of marriage, the partners enumerate all the circumstances that may occur in their union ("for better or worse, for richer or poorer, in sickness and in health"), and each promises, through it all, to love and cherish the other. The commitment is then sealed by the pledge "and thereto I plight [meaning offer in pledge] thee my faith."[3] In more recent versions of the ritual for marriage, of course, the language has been modified. Yet the service retains the notion that the partners in marriage are offering to one another, regardless of the circumstances they may encounter, the full measure of their faith, which is understood as trust, loyalty, and commitment.

> **Pledged faith is the doorway to further discovery and knowledge.**

Faith understood in this context of trust, love, and commitment may provide an analogy for the role of faith similarly understood in our knowledge of God. In the service of marriage, to be sure, there is an element of knowledge *about* the other.

---

3   From *The Methodist Hymnal* (Nashville: Methodist Publishing House, 1939).

Couples naturally learn about the other and his or her values and background. Pastors and counselors may even encourage them to take inventory of their attitudes, values, and lifestyle choices in arriving at a decision to marry and to discuss it with one another. But at the heart of the matter as they pledge their faith to one another is the commitment each makes to love the other and to be loyal to the other regardless of the circumstances. In the security of that commitment, they are free to be vulnerable and to share the depths of their spirits with the other. The faith that is pledged is a necessary condition for coming to know the one to whom they are wed. Terry Eagleton, British literary critic, put it this way: "It is only by having faith in someone that we can take the risk of disclosing ourselves to him or her fully, thus making true knowledge of ourselves possible."[4] In human relationships, pledged faith is the doorway to further discovery and knowledge.

There are parallels to this faith in the soaring assurance Saint Paul gave to the Christians in Rome concerning their standing in God's love. He enumerated the struggle that goes on within the individual between the perfect will of God and our feeble moral efforts. In Romans 8:38-39 he listed all the human and cosmic adversaries that might create a divide between us and God. He lists ten factors that might attempt to create this alienation from the divine (death, life, angels, rulerships, things present, things to come, powers, height, depth, and any other creature). Following that listing he then assured his Christian friends that they could

---

4   Terry Eagleton, *Reason, Faith, and Revolution: Reflections on the God Debate* (New Haven, CT: Yale University Press, 2009), 121.

remain secure in that love despite all their adversaries.[5] Nothing could separate them from the love of God in Christ Jesus.

{ Nothing separates us from the love of God. }

Faith, Language of the Heart

It is clear from the discussion to this point that the language of faith is more than a carefully weighed judgment about the likelihood of a Being—in addition to the world around us—who is referred to as God. No covenant partners stand at the altar and solemnly agree that the other exists! That is assumed, of course, but the *existence* of the other is not a matter of solemn vows. What *is* at stake is the relationship of trust, commitment, and loyalty that they pledge to one another. The pledge to take the other for a wife or husband is sometimes called *performative language*, meaning that it is language that enacts what it declares. "I take you to be my wedded wife/husband" does not merely provide information; it establishes a new relationship.

Faith in God is a comprehensive response of the whole person to the Ultimate Reality, the Source of all life. The Bible speaks of knowing and loving God in the language of the heart. The Shema, the ancient prayer of Israel (Deuteronomy 6:4-5), enjoins the believer to love God "with all your heart, and with all your soul, and with all your might." In the book of Jeremiah, God gave the prophet a vision of life beyond the imminent ruin that Israel was to

------

5   See Robert Jewett, *Romans: A Commentary* (Minneapolis: Fortress Press, 2007), 554.

suffer in the form of the exile, and through Jeremiah, God made a promise to Israel: "I will give them a heart to know that I am the LORD (24:7). God further promised to write the new covenant on the hearts of the people. No longer would they need to be reminded to know the Lord, "for they shall all know me, from the least of them to the greatest" (31:34).

Jeremiah's emphasis on "a heart to know" reminds us that in the Bible each organ of the body has symbolic meaning. In our world, the heart is primarily the seat of human emotion and striving. In the biblical world, the heart also had a role in thinking and reasoning. The heart was a key to understanding humans as rational beings. A text in Deuteronomy declares: "But to this day, the LORD has not given you a heart to understand or eyes to see or ears to hear" (29:4 ESV). This suggests that the heart, eyes, and ears are three different organs through which we reach out and interpret our world.[6]

In practical atheism we see that denial of God is not solely or even primarily a matter of faulty thinking. It is "abominable deeds," the conduct of life as if God were not sovereign, that prompts the label of "fool" for the one who denies God (Psalm 14:1). Jesus reflects a similar understanding in the parable of the rich fool (Luke 12:13-21). The peril that befell the rich fool was not because his thinking was mixed up. It was a corrupt heart that prompted him to center his security in his possessions and to focus his life on consumption that preceded his fall. He was termed a fool because by his actions he denied that God exists.

---

6   See Katharine Doob Sakenfeld, ed., *The New Interpreter's Dictionary of the Bible* (Nashville: Abingdon Press, 2007), 2:764.

Perhaps it was the realization of this meaning of "fool" that prompted the British literary critic Terry Eagleton to express himself as he did. He writes of the atheism that finds many adherents in the contemporary world. It is not merely a question of God's existence that is at stake, he insists. If God should place upon the skies in mile-high letters the words "I'M UP HERE, YOU IDIOTS!" that announcement alone would not necessarily make any difference on matters of faith. Faith involves more than additional information. Faith represents "a radical transformation of what we say and do."[7] Faith is a matter of the heart, a context for the living of a life, and not merely a proposition confirmed by the head.

Faith, Trust, and Mystery

The novelist Flannery O'Connor once wrote that mystery is an embarrassment to the modern mind.[8] We have seen how René Descartes (1596–1650) attempted to base religious belief on an unshakable foundation, the existence of the thinking self. No one could deny the self without self-contradiction. And this, Descartes believed, removed any element of mystery from religious belief. On this foundation he built his system of clear and distinct ideas. At the end of his book on method, he made an amazing statement in defiance of mystery. He expressed the hope that "those who have understood all that has been said . . . will . . . see nothing whose cause they cannot easily understand or anything

---

7   Eagleton, *Reason, Faith, and Revolution*, 113.
8   Referred to in Harvey Cox, *The Future of Faith* (New York: HarperOne, 2009), 22

that gives them any reason to marvel."[9] In the decades and centuries that have followed, it has been characteristic of our modern mind-set to regard unfathomable mysteries as problems to be solved. If there is a problem to which we have no answer at the present, it has been customary to believe that an answer will be found in the future through science.

Flying in the face of this stance is the concept of mystery, which is not something that we eliminate by finding a simple answer or solution. Mystery, in the words of French philosopher Gabriel Marcel (1889–1973), is "something in which I find myself caught up, and whose essence is not before me in its entirety."[10] This view of mystery is consistent with the expression of Albert Einstein that we referred to in chapter 2. There, instead of representing a barrier to be eliminated, Einstein termed the mysterious as fundamental and "the cradle of all art and science." One who can no longer stand in rapt awe before the world, said Einstein, is as "good as dead."

Religious faith is founded on radical trust in what is fundamentally mysterious. That is to say, religious faith is directed at Ultimate Reality, "what lasts when everything else is gone," as Dinah put it in George Eliot's novel *Adam Bede*. We also express faith, to be sure, in objects that are less than final. We say we have faith or trust in the rule of law, the loyalty of a friend, the skill of a surgeon, and so on. All this is understandable. But religious faith in its depth is radical trust in Ultimate Reality, the unfathomable Source of

---

9   René Descartes, *On Method, Optics, Geometry, and Meteorology*, trans. P. J. Olscamp (Indianapolis: Bobbs-Merrill, 1965), 361.

10   Gabriel Marcel, *Being and Having* (London: Marcel Press, 1965), 101.

life at its origins and its Destiny at the last. This Ultimate Reality is the force that we cannot "define." We cannot delimit it. It is not a problem to be solved. It is a mystery in which we live. To place our trust in this final mystery, the ultimate context in which we live, is the last step in faith.

We have to sympathize with Job when he put his case before God and attempted to fit what had befallen him into neat categories. Perhaps we even cheer for Job in his well-known statement of his case before God. But at the end, Job was forced to concede his case and bow in trust, affirming to the Lord:

> I know that you can do all things,
>   and that no purpose of yours can be thwarted . . .
>
> Therefore I have uttered what I did not understand,
>   things too wonderful for me, which I did not know . . .
>
> I had heard of you by the hearing of the ear,
>   but now my eye sees you;
> therefore, I despise myself,
>   and repent in dust and ashes. (Job 42:2-6)

Job faced into the mystery and recognized that he had no categories by which he could comprehend what had befallen him. He recognized that his attempts to do so had been shown to be impossible. What he was forced by experience to do was to believe in and trust what he could not understand.

When we speak of faith as trust, then, we are not referring to an attempt on our part to formulate standards of trustworthiness and then measure God against those standards, eventually concluding that the Almighty is to be trusted. Rather, we are suggesting that we look into the face of mystery and rely on the Final Reality in order to be directed toward our good. Furthermore, we understand that the goodness of God does not mean that God conforms to our standards of goodness but that whatever God wills is good.[11]

Several practical results flow from this posture of faith. First, the conviction that, whatever the appearances, God is good and that God's will is directed toward our good gives us bearing in difficult times. The author of 1 Peter in the New Testament addresses Christians who were undergoing a fiery ordeal. He urges them, in the midst of suffering, to "cast all your anxiety on [God], because he cares for you" (5:7). The way Christians affirm radical trust in God is in the pattern of their lives. The radical trust of which we speak authorizes a person to act based on the conviction Saint Paul shared with the Christians in Rome: "We know that in all things God works for the good of those who love him, who have been called according to his purpose" (Romans 8:28 NIV). To act on the basis of God's goodness is a way of affirming the goodness of God, as attested in the Bible, even if we cannot pretend to comprehend the full meaning of the intrinsic goodness of God.[12]

The second result that flows from faith as radical trust is that faith contributes to further understanding. Anselm of Canterbury (1033–1109) spoke of "faith seeking understanding." The act of believing and trusting in God's goodness gives us a basis for understanding God's action in a deeper context. We can see a parallel to

---

11 See this perspective in George A. Lindbeck, *The Nature of Doctrine: Religion and Theology in a Postliberal Age* (Philadelphia: Westminster Press, 1984), 66–67.

12 Ibid., 67.

this in our own human relationships. One who trusts and relies on a friend or a spouse does not verify that trust by constant loyalty checks or surveillance. The corrosive nature of that scrutiny runs counter to the trust supposedly invested in another. A good friend or spouse acts on the basis of trust. We trust enough to become vulnerable to the other, and in this situation of vulnerability we find the worthiness of that trust is confirmed. To stake everything on the goodness of God and act on the basis that God is trustworthy and that one day that trustworthiness will be confirmed is to place oneself in a context for confirming that this trust is well placed. Life experience corroborates the confidence placed in God.

A Witness to Faith

I witnessed the power of this radical trust in the goodness of God in the life of a good friend and colleague as he and his wife experienced the death of their daughter, then a young adult beginning a career in law. I, the two parents, and their pastor stood in their kitchen just after hearing the word that their daughter had been struck by a bus in a city five hours away and was critically injured. We stood in a circle while the parents reported bits of information they had received from the hospital to which their severely injured daughter was taken. The bus had made a left turn into the pedestrian walkway. Their daughter, who had the right-of-way, was struck by the bus and dragged beneath it. The physicians were doing everything they could for her, but the prospects were grim.

We held hands in that kitchen and prayed together. With tears the father simply said, "Whatever happens, we're going to trust God." He later said that he wasn't sure from where that instant affirmation came. But he said it again, "Whatever happens, we're going to trust God." The parents left their home and began a torturous drive through Friday evening traffic in one city and made their way to their daughter's bedside. The daughter's condition did not improve, and within twenty-four hours they had no option but to concede the worst and remove her from life support. Her death took place on her father's birthday and the day before Mother's Day.

The parents recognized that the death of their daughter was the result of human negligence and error. Her death was heartbreaking, but their faith led them to know first that God shared their heartbreak. Second, they expected, even in their grief, that God would work for good even in that grim catastrophe. Following the desire their daughter had expressed earlier in her life, they immediately made the decision to donate her organs to individuals awaiting an organ transplant. The parents and a surviving daughter became advocates to spread word of the need for organ donations. They spoke at public forums on organ donation. Later, they received a note from the recipient of their daughter's heart telling them that because of their donation, he had seen another sunrise.

Because of their confidence that God was working for good even in the midst of their anguish, they organized a scholarship fund at the university from which their daughter had graduated. This fund was to assist future students in work missions to third-world countries. Work colleagues and friends of the deceased through Habitat for Humanity built a house in their community for a well-qualified family, donating money and physical labor to provide shelter for someone who would have otherwise been without housing.

My colleague, the father, then wrote a textbook on responding to loss, and he used that textbook along with other resources to offer courses at a theological seminary to prepare future pastors and counselors to help others in confronting loss in the context of faith and trust. He initiated a group made up of fathers who had lost a child, and that original group expanded to form other circles of mourning fathers. That group wrote a book describing their losses and how they were responding to them.[13] Now, twenty years after this catastrophic loss, the father has written yet another book that is circulating widely through church discussion groups. He titled it *Three Simple Truths*. The chapter headings for the three simple truths say it all:

"God Is Good, All the Time"
"God Works for Good, in Everything"
"Trust God, No Matter What."[14]

The point, of course, is not to diminish in any way the enormous loss and anguish experienced by this family in the death of their daughter. What this experience and the family's response to it do illustrate is the trust that guided their response to that loss. Their trust was translated into action. Their expectation that God was working for good even in this catastrophe led them to be alert to ways that good could be expressed. Their deep faith in the

---

13 *Tuesday Mornings with the Dads: Stories by Fathers Who Have Lost a Son or a Daughter* (Portland, OR: Inkwater Press, 2009).

14 Adolf Hansen, *Three Simple Truths: Experiencing Them in Our Lives* (Portland, OR: Inkwater Press, 2014). His previous book was *Responding to Loss: A Resource for Caregivers* (Amityville, NY: Baywood, 2004).

goodness of God endowed them with vision and expectation that made some good come even from devastating loss.

> { Faith in the goodness of God becomes the lens through which we see more deeply. }

Faith and Vision

Faith as a fundamental trust in the goodness of God becomes the lens through which we see the world. We have seen in chapter 2 that anything we can know about the world that is worth knowing is known through interpretation. Options are available, of course. One can adopt the stance that the world is senseless and pointless and that blind fate determines our passage through this life. That perspective will shape the expectations we have of life, and such expectations are likely to be confirmed. The scientist, likewise, can adopt the expectation that the world reflects order and law, and this faith perspective will likely be rewarded by further discovery of the way that order and law are manifest.

Faith as trust represents a set of perspectives. It is a resolution to conduct oneself in the confidence that certain truths are trustworthy and in the assurance that they will one day be confirmed. It is a posture that is confirmed by the possibilities it opens in the present and by the confident hope it engenders for the time to come.

REFLECTION QUESTIONS

1. Is Eagleton right that a sign in the sky would not in itself give us faith? If we could prove God's existence, would that settle the question of faith? What more, in your view, is required?

2. In what way is "pledging of one's faith" in a wedding parallel to faith in God? How do you respond to the suggestion that trust is essential in knowing another person well?

3. How would you explain to one who is not a believer what Jeremiah meant when he wrote of a "heart to know" God (Jeremiah 24:7) or what Deuteronomy means where it speaks of "a heart to understand, or eyes to see, or ears to hear" (29:4)? How is knowing with the head similar to or different from knowing with the heart?

4. What does it mean to say that something is not a problem to be solved but rather a mystery in which we live? What does it mean to speak of God as a mystery?

5. How did the trust of the parents in the face of their daughter's death affect the consequences that issued from this catastrophe? How would lack of trust on their part have led to other consequences?

6. How would you describe the change in outlook that is reflected in Job's statement in Job 42:2-6? Have you ever been required to undergo a similar change in outlook?

Origins of Faith

Where can I go from your spirit?
*   Or where can I flee from your presence?*
                    —Psalm 139:7

There is an element of faith involved in anything we can know, and trust in and reliance upon God are at the core of religious faith. This naturally raises the question of the origins of such faith. Why is it that some can affirm their trust in God even during catastrophic loss, while others lack anything resembling this trust in the circumstances of their lives?

It is necessary to maintain a certain modesty in trying to understand why some have such faith and others do not. In religious circles we often speak of faith as a gift of God. An anthropologist reminds us that faith as trust is not something to be gained by sheer willpower. "Universal trust in life is like a mood that comes over a person and fills his life with gladness, revealing meaning and value where previously there seemed to be only the empty desert of absolute pointlessness.'"[1] Trusting faith is a gift that conveys a basic sense of security.

The Advent of Trust

Specialists in child development stress the importance of an infant learning to trust his or her surroundings. The love of the parents is essential for the child to grow physically as well as emotionally. Children who are denied that love, it has been shown, may suffer weight loss, sleeplessness, and arrested development. Childhood specialists remind us that newborns learn very quickly how to relate to their circumstances and to expect the immediate environment to be secure and nurturing. They learn quite soon to identify their mother by scent. They learn to focus their eyes at a distance, which allows them to recognize their mother's face when they are nursing. They soon recognize and respond to facial expressions and are much more interested in the human face than they are in other objects placed before them. Before words have meaning, the mere sound of the mother or another family member conveys comfort and security. A child can recognize the sound of his or her mother tongue—as opposed to other languages—by the age of six months. Through all the early weeks of life, the infant finds comfort and security in being held and talked to or sung to. Newborns come to expect a response that soothes and nurtures when they cry in the night. This essential trust in the mother and father gradually expands into a trust in life itself.

---

1   Otto Bollnow, quoted in Hans Küng, *Does God Exist?: An Answer for Today*, trans. Edward Quinn (Garden City, NY: Doubleday, 1980), 452.

Maintaining and growing in trust are requirements for social interaction and growth in the maturing adult. As the individual matures, this basic trust develops into faith to the extent that the individual is assured that this trust is not groundless, that it is not without a foundation in reality. H. Richard Niebuhr described this growing faith as "the attitude of the self in its existence toward all existences that surround it, as beings to be relied upon or suspected. It is," he continued, "trust or distrust in being itself."[2] To note that this fundamental trust is often prompted by a loving and supportive set of surroundings is not, however, to suggest that these circumstances by themselves instill a sense of security in fundamental reality. Some individuals who were denied such a context in their early childhood nonetheless become people of faith as adults.

Trust of this fundamental nature occurs—or fails to occur—without a conscious decision on our part. Terry Eagleton reminds us, "It is more common to find oneself believing something than to make a conscious decision to do so—or at least to make such a conscious decision because you find yourself leaning that way already." Faith, he contends, is a "question of being gripped by a commitment from which one finds oneself unable to walk away."[3]

At this point, it is well to recognize that our growth and identity as people who hold certain beliefs is not an individual affair, or even just an interaction between ourselves and a loving and nurturing parent. From birth we enter a world constituted by those who went before. Those who preceded us have created a society in relation

---

2   H. Richard Niebuhr, *The Responsible Self: An Essay in Christian Moral Philoso-phy*, new ed. (Louisville: Westminster John Knox Press, 1999), 118.

3   Eagleton, *Reason, Faith, and Revolution*, 137 (see chap. 4, n. 4).

to which we become the people we are. At birth we are presented with a social order that includes a language, a set of rules, moral maxims, folk stories, and a variety of other guidelines that define a social order. This social order, this society, is presented to us as we interact with others. We learn to speak according to certain grammatical rules. We learn in interaction with others the roles we are to play, the rules that govern those roles, and the stories that outline what is allowable in our society and what is proscribed.

Our development as selves, according to this theory, takes place in interaction with the humanly constructed social order and culture into which we are born. Humans create this social and cultural order, and this order is projected as "the way things are." This social construction represents a projected structure comparable in standing to the natural and physical world that surrounds us. Finally, members of the society are led to appropriate or internalize the rules and maxims of the social order as if it were "second nature." The social order has coercive ways of enforcing those understandings. Those who fail to conform are censored, scorned, or punished. The root meaning for "idiot" is in the Greek word *idios*, meaning "personal," "distinct" or "one who stands apart." The person denoted by such derisive terms is one who is marked as standing apart from the approved structures of that society.[4]

However we may respond to this theory of our social structure, we can scarcely deny that we are inherently social creatures. We are born into and grow and develop not solely as individuals

---

4   For an outline of the socialization of the individual and the role of religions in undergirding a theistic construction of the universe, see Peter L. Berger, *The Sacred Canopy: Elements of a Sociological Theory of Religion* (New York: Doubleday, 1967), chaps. 1 and 2.

but as members of a society and culture that we inherit. If this is true of our identity with our social order, it is also true of our relationship with what is ultimate in meaning—the sacred or divine. As we develop, we confront in varying degrees not only a given order for our human society but an account of transcendent reality. That Transcendent Reality, God, is depicted as the awesome and finally mysterious power by which we come to be. In its most basic terms, we speak of God as the One under whose will we live and over whom we have no control. God in these terms is the ultimate limit for our lives.

As we shall see, individuals may differ in the manner and context in which they relate to this final or ultimate awesome power. Some may regard this power as capricious, uncaring and purposeless. Others may relate to this Final Power as infinite in love and redeeming care. At this stage the issue is not the question of the existence or nonexistence of this power over life. Every human faces it.

Psalm 139 presents the abiding reality that in the midst of life, there is One who is inescapable. "Where can I go from your spirit?" our writer asks (v. 7). The psalmist describes the extreme locations to which one might flee. One might go to the edges of the earth, to the farthest expanse of the sea (v. 8). Surely that would be the test of God's reach, for the sea was thought to be a place of chaos and disorder. (Creation took place in the Genesis narrative, we should remember, only when God had instituted order over the depths and divided them from the dry lands.) Then the psalmist said that he could ascend into heaven or descend into hell. Still God's presence would encircle him (v. 9). Finally, the writer tells us that he could clothe himself in dense darkness and in that place of abandonment he would find that there is no darkness in God, for "darkness is as light to you" (vv. 11-12). Again, the message of the psalm is not to speculate on the possibility of God's existence. This psalm testifies that God is the Final Reality who knows us thoroughly, and, far from representing merely an option for life, is the inescapable and final power who is to be acknowledged by all flesh.

Revealing Events

It is basic to faith to hold that certain events are particularly transparent to the nature of this ultimate power that surrounds our lives. Certain happenings, according to faith, give us insight into the nature of God. Alfred North Whitehead wrote, "Rational religion appeals to the direct intuition of special occasions, and to the elucidatory power of its concepts for all occasions."[5] Certain happenings convey a disclosure of God that sheds light on all we experience.

The disclosure of meaning through events should remind us that this is not unlike the way we know other people. People we know often have characteristic expressions, facial cues, patterns of speech, or other ways by which we identify their characters and personalities. In ways of which we may be unaware, a certain smile or gesture will convey something about a person's character. When two people fall in love, there is a special way of seeing that enables one individual to interpret another in a manner not available to passing acquaintances. Others may say, "I don't know what

---

5   From Alfred North Whitehead's *Religion in the Making,* quoted in H. Richard Niebuhr, *The Meaning of Revelation* (New York: Macmillan, 1962), 93.

she sees in him" as a way of acknowledging that there is a special insight available to one individual that is not shared by another. This special insight is not reducible to a neutral or dispassionate interpretation of the one who is known. It refers to a close relationship in which the character and soul of one person is revealed to another.

Similarly, special events reveal elements of another person that are not recognized in the ordinary sequence of events. I grew up admiring my father for many traits, including his courage and his care for others. I learned this truth about him through my childhood and teenage years. On one occasion when I was away from home at college, I picked up the newspaper from my hometown about fifty miles away. There on the front page was a picture of my father. He was not dressed in his normal suit and tie. His work clothes were in some disarray. The picture accompanied a story about his rescue of a neighbor from a home near him. A gas line had exploded in that home, and in the aftermath there was the threat of further explosions. The story recounted that before any first responders could arrive, my father had entered the home at considerable risk to himself and searched for survivors. He found a neighbor who was alive but injured, and he carried her through the flames to safety, undoubtedly saving her life. The courage and compassion shown in that event disclosed who he was in unforgettable form. The qualities that defined who he was were always there, but they were particularly evident in that special event.

Whether we are speaking of dramatic lifesaving events or discernment of a characteristic smile, the revelation we gain of others represents the coincidence of an event and an interpretation. The particular smile of a close friend may communicate to us his or her sense of humor. A heroic act is not only an event initiated by another but a disclosure of enduring courage and bravery.

In the Bible we confront a series of events in which men and women of faith testify to disclosures of the divine. These encounters cast illuminating power over all their history. Jacob sleeps at Bethel and dreams of a ladder reaching into heaven. He hears a voice from God issuing a promise. When Jacob awakes from the dream, he interprets it as a disclosure of the divine. "Surely the LORD is in this place—and I did not know it" (Genesis 28:16). When Joseph's brothers, having bound him and sold him to traders, come to him after he becomes the chief administrator for Pharaoh in Egypt and ask for food, Joseph interprets their treachery toward him as a part of God's plan for the welfare of the family. His brothers meant their betrayal of him for ill, but God uses it for good (Genesis 50:20). Moses stepped aside and beheld a bush that was aflame and yet was not consumed. He sensed that he was on holy ground and there heard God's call and commission (Exodus 3).

All these—and a succession of revealing events that extend through the whole biblical witness—are events that are interpreted in faith as disclosures of the Holy One who sees, hears, and comes to deliver. In the New Testament the first witnesses of Jesus's life, death, and resurrection testify to events through which God shows divine love and redemptive power, the victory over death in raising Jesus from the dead. The apostles who bear witness to these events assure their hearers that the Christ who showed himself alive to many brothers and sisters is present in power with them as well.

Tradition and Stories

When we link witnesses to these revealing events into an inclusive account of the history of a people, a narrative, we have a tradition that forms and shapes a truth-seeking community in the midst of history. Individuals have encounters with a presence that they interpret to be with the Holy One. They link their encounter to the stories that are told by others. They conclude that they are experiencing the Holy One again. Their collective stories form an inclusive narrative that conveys God's purposes in their history and the direction toward which God is leading them.

The truth of the matter is that we live our lives through stories.[6] When meeting another for the first time, we become acquainted with the individual through exchanging stories. We recite for one another where we live, the makeup of our family, the work in which we engage, and perhaps something about our present activities. We have a basis for relating through exchanging stories of our lives.

Whenever families that are otherwise separated by distances get together, they affirm the ties that bind by recitation of events that have taken place in the family. Sometimes the stories will relate the habits and lovable traits of family members who are no longer with them. They will recall events in the life of a grandfather or an aunt that will bring that loved one back into the family circle once more. They will rehearse early antics of the childhood of family members who are now adults. Stories may be recited

______

6   See this emphasis in Alasdair MacIntyre, *After Virtue*, 2nd ed. (Notre Dame, IN: Notre Dame Press, 1984), 212.

almost as a ritual. One member of my family used to preface a favorite story by saying, "If you have heard this before, don't stop me. I want to hear it again." We celebrate ties and relationships through narratives.

Furthermore, it is through narratives that we understand others. In interpreting their actions or attitudes, we may place them in a credible narrative of their lives. If we see a woman loudly and sternly speaking to a child at a curb on a busy city street, for example, we do not necessarily leap to the conclusion that the woman is a grouch and is verbally harassing the child. We are more likely to recognize that the woman is a loving mother who is expressing her love by impressing, albeit loudly, upon the child that she is not to cross the street without waiting for the light and looking carefully in both directions. We make sense out of her actions by interpreting them in the context of a credible story.

Howard Thurman, former dean of Marsh Chapel at Boston University, was a poet, mystic, and preacher. He was also the grandson of a slave. His grandmother as a young woman had lived as a slave on a plantation. When Thurman was a youngster, his elderly grandmother told him stories about enduring life as a slave. She often told stories of the plantation church. The owner allowed the slaves to get together on Sundays out under a tree in the fields. One of the slaves, an elderly man, served as the preacher each time they met. Thurman's grandmother said that their preacher's sermons were never complete until they had "gone by Calvary." The preacher would recite the account that they knew well of a good man who was vilified, scorned by the people in power, tortured and humiliated by a mocking crowd, and who breathed his last accompanied by the derision of the crowd. His congregation knew what it was to suffer pain and humiliation and to feel forsaken. Then the preacher, having recited the pain and degradation of that Friday, recounted the story of Easter morning: how God had raised up the good man from the dead and had taken the One who was forsaken and despised and seated him at God's right hand.

Thurman's grandmother then triumphantly told him that, at that point in the story, the preacher would take off his spectacles, look into the eyes of his congregation, and say: "Just remember: You are not slaves. You are not anybody's property. You are children of God." And Dean Thurman added, "When my grandmother got to that part of her story, there would be slight stiffening in her spine as we sucked in our breath. When she had finished, our spirits were restored."[7] The story had reminded her, contrary to all the oppressive conditions of slavery, of the person she really was in God's eyes.

This account illustrates the way the Bible portrays a succession of events, an inclusive narrative, that outlines the context in which we live. Through these pivotal events in the Old and New Testaments, the person of faith gains a picture of what is fundamentally real, who God is and what God is doing. In consequence, believers have a deepened sense of self about what they are to do with the one life that God gives.

---

7   Howard Thurman, *With Head and Heart: The Autobiography of Howard Thurman* (New York: Harcourt Brace Jovanovich, 1979), 21.

Communities of Interpretation

The church is a community that understands itself and its world by means of a story that is proclaimed. Other communities are shaped by their own narratives. For example, John Polkinghorne compares the church assembled around key events to the scientific community in which he participates. Those communities are likewise organized around formative events—in this case a history of controlled experiments—and they interpret reality through the lens of the realities disclosed in those experiments. To be sure, the recital of God's doings in the Bible is not strictly comparable to a controlled laboratory experiment. According to Polkinghorne, however, both are examples of truth-seeking communities that interpret reality by interrelating a history of events with their present experience. In different ways both communities may contend that the history of events around which they are organized brings them into contact with what is fundamentally real about the world.[8]

We have noted that sociologists tell us we live in a world that is socially constructed. It includes a language with rules of usage, a prescription of roles, and a set of standards by which life is to be lived. Living as a member of a society involves reckoning and to some measure internalizing this social construction. To step significantly outside of this socially constructed reality is to confront meaninglessness or chaos.

Religious communities, while they are voluntary societies, likewise define the way the world is. They interpret the world through

---

8   John Polkinghorne, "Faith in God the Creator," in *Belief: Readings on the Reason for Faith*, ed. Francis S. Collins (New York: HarperCollins, 2010), 199–200.

narratives embedded in sacred texts. The Scriptures, as acknowledged by the community, outline and describe a realm of reality,
the sacred, that transcends but nonetheless interrelates with the
mundane and its history. The world is interpreted as the creation
of a loving God, and the purposes and intentions of this God are
known through events as they are interpreted by the community.
Becoming a member of this community of faith involves not only
an acceptance of this biblical narrative but proficiency in interpreting the world through that understanding. The slave community described by Howard Thurman embraced the story of Calvary
as the depiction of God's redeeming love for them. The listeners
grasped the true significance of their situation by interpreting it
through the story.

Earlier I mentioned those who refer to themselves as "spiritual
but not religious." Often the "religion" such individuals have dis-
owned is the doctrinal, traditional, and institutional expression of
faith. While we can respect these sentiments, we must note that
they significantly underestimate the social structure of our faith as
it develops. In our Western culture we often think of ourselves as
individualists in matters of faith, as well as in other aspects of our
lives. We sometimes hear parents speak of forgoing any religious
instruction for their children, so they can "figure it out for themselves" when they grow up and then decide what religion, if any,
they will embrace.

But many of us will respond that we do not form our faith
and our perspective on the world as individuals. We embrace and
interact with the world in the light of and with the use of traditions. Some have pointed out that our religious traditions are
conversations and arguments over time that are questioned and

refined in the light of experience. Job, for example, clearly challenged the tradition that his suffering was prompted by a hidden sin for which he must repent (Job 21:17-26). Ezekiel contradicted the notion that we are punished for the sins of those who have gone before (Ezekiel 18:1-4). Jesus revised the prescription of an eye for an eye (Matthew 5:38-42). A tradition, thus, does not merely transmit wisdom gained during the course of living a story; rather, it sharpens and refines the story in the light of ongoing experience.

Our predisposition is to assume that tradition cannot be a carrier of truth. But such a view is now coming under serious review. The late Edward Farley, renowned theology professor, for example, spoke for many when he noted, "The philosophy and sociology of science today argue that all knowledge occurs in conjunction with deposits and strands of tradition, and this includes sciences."[9] The application of this to scientific studies was illustrated extensively by physicist and historian Thomas Kuhn more than fifty years ago. According to his analysis, scientific research takes place in the context of scientific traditions, or paradigms, as he termed them. It is through the tradition or paradigm that our questions for research are formed. When results begin to cast doubt upon the prevailing paradigm, he wrote, a series of questions is asked about it. If questions cannot be answered in the context of that paradigm, then there is need to search for a new paradigm, which itself becomes the basis for scientific research. Such a "scientific revolution," as Kuhn termed it, took place in the overthrow of the Ptolemaic view

---

9   Edward Farley, *The Fragility of Knowledge: Theological Education in the Church and the University* (Philadelphia: Fortress Press, 1988), 8.

in which the earth was pictured at the center of the universe. This view was modified, after copious efforts to preserve the old, into the new, Copernican view of the universe, which viewed the sun as the center.[10]

In reflecting on the origins of faith, we are impressed with the way we know ourselves and relate to our world through the influence of stories. We gain our identity by acknowledging which story we are a part of. We evaluate an action based on its fit or lack of fit with that story. When we become a part of a community of faith, we accept that community's story as the significant measure of the universe in which we live. We assess potential lines of action according to our answer to the question, "Of what story do I find myself a part?" Thus, the people of Israel were called to account for themselves not strictly speaking by a creed but by the recital of a story: "A wandering Aramean was my ancestor; he went down into Egypt and lived there as an alien, few in number, and there he became a great nation, mighty and populous" (Deuteronomy 26:5). This witness was followed by a recital of events through which the Lord delivered the people from the oppressive hand of Pharaoh.

The name of Ruby Bridges came to the foreground during the early civil rights struggle in the United States. In 1960, when the public schools were integrated in New Orleans, six-year-old Ruby became the first African-American child to attend her school. White parents withdrew their children from the school in protest. Sixty-five National Guard troops were assigned to

---

10 Thomas S. Kuhn, *The Structure of Scientific Revolutions*, 2nd ed. (Chicago: University of Chicago Press, 1970), 68–69, 72.

protect Ruby against the two hundred members of the white community who formed outside the school in protest on the first day. When Ruby arrived, protesters called out hate slogans, death threats, and racial slurs. Remarkably, Ruby endured this incredible duress and entered her school. As she walked through the crowd of protesters, her teacher noticed that her lips were moving. The teacher later asked her to whom she was talking. Ruby answered that she was talking to God. When asked what she was saying, she said she was asking God to forgive the people who were so mean to her.

Robert Coles, a professor at Harvard, was studying children of the poor when he learned of Ruby's story. He marveled that this child could bear such stress without developing serious psychological problems. The Bridges family lived in modest circumstances, and neither of Ruby's parents could read or write. Coles arranged to talk with Ruby in the kitchen of her home. He told her that her teacher had told him about her lips moving as she passed through the threatening mob. "What were you saying?" he asked. She repeated that she had been praying for the people. When Coles asked her what she had said to God, she replied that she prayed each day for God to forgive them, because they didn't know what they were doing.

The Bridges family could not afford therapy. They had not studied the stages of moral reasoning, nor had they done a literary study of the New Testament. But they had memorized passages of Scripture from the Old and New Testaments. Their minister had quoted Jesus's words from the cross. At a very early age, Ruby had embraced and lived in the light of that tradition in an extraordinary manner. She engaged in a practice that brought the wisdom of ancient tradition into a critical passage of her life.[11] Philosopher Alasdair MacIntyre might have had such a story in mind when he said, "Children learn or mislearn what a child and what a parent is, what the cast of characters may be in the drama into which they have been born and what the ways of the world are. Deprive children of stories and you leave them unscripted, anxious stutterers in their actions as in their words."[12]

Conclusion

We have seen that the origins for faith begin with our first breaths. The conditions for faith grow as we interact with the social construction of reality that surrounds us and with the stories and traditions by which we interpret the world. In later chapters we will look further into the refinement of faith through shared, revealing events, traditions, and practices of faith. In the next chapter we will focus on the narrative by which the Christian faith is understood—the life, death, and resurrection of Jesus Christ.

REFLECTION QUESTIONS

1. How do you respond to the affirmation in Psalm 139 that God knows the thoughts of our minds and our words even before they are on our lips? In your view is it good news, or a threat, to be known so well?

---

11 "Robert Coles on Ruby Bridges," YouTube video, 5:23, interview, posted by Colette Ouattara, May 5, 2013, https://www.youtube.com/watch?v=XPK 3zQM2dHU.
12 MacIntyre, *After Virtue*, 216.

2. Can you think of any events that disclosed someone's character to you? How did that affect your estimate of him or her?

3. If someone asked you to tell your life story, which events would you include? By what story would you like to be known by others?

4. The narrative of Jesus's crucifixion gave the young Ruby Bridges guidance in responding to angry crowds. Are there stories from the Bible or elsewhere that have been guides for you? What title would a filmmaker give to the story of your life?

5. Can you think of stories that distinguish your family or circle of friends? Are they repeated at family reunions or meetings with friends after a long absence? In what ways do the biblical stories function in a comparable way when the believing community gathers?

Faith and God Made Known

*Jesus is both a mirror to our humanity and a window to divinity,
a window revealing as much of God as is given mortal eyes to see.*[1]

—William Sloane Coffin

*No one has ever seen God;
it is the only Son, who is nearest to the Father's heart,
who has made him known.*

—John 1:18 (Jerusalem Bible)

In our discussion to this point, we have stood in some wonderment at the thirst for meaning and permanence that resides within us. It is all the more remarkable that we humans, creatures who, as we noted, arrived on our planet only three seconds before midnight, were created only a little lower than God and have been crowned with glory and honor (Psalm 8:5). Our lives represent only a momentary blip in the incomprehensible 13.7 billion years of our universe. We reside on a planet among the 100 billion or so

---

1   William Sloane Coffin, *Credo* (Louisville: John Knox Press, 2014), 12.

stars in our galaxy, which is itself only one of the more than 100 billion galaxies in the universe we have observed so far.

The Old Testament record makes it clear that we are not to see God as we see other individuals. When Moses, the prototype of prophet and priest, first asked to see God's glory, God told him, "You cannot see my face; for no one shall see me and live" (Exodus 33:20). Yet God allowed Moses to stand in the cleft of a rock while God passed by, showing Moses only God's back (v. 23). The people of Israel, we are told, saw God by the presence of a cloud on the tabernacle during the day and as a fire by night (40:38). Only at the end of the Pentateuch, the first five books of the Bible, is Moses lauded for his singular relationship with God: "Never since has there arisen a prophet in Israel like Moses, whom the LORD knew face to face" (Deuteronomy 34:10). Moses clearly stood alone in terms of his access to God.

There are interesting parallels between Moses's quest to see the glory of God and the contemporary scientific search for a unified theory, the TOE, or "theory of everything" that would integrate our understanding of the fundamental forces of the universe. Though Albert Einstein was not a believer in a traditional sense, he phrased his search in strikingly theological terms: "I want to know how God created this world. I'm not interested in this or that phenomenon, in the spectrum of this or that element. I want to know his thoughts. The rest are details."[2] He spoke often of his admiration for the intellectual ingenuity of the universe, the mathematic elegance of its workings, and he suggested that

---

2   E. Salaman, "A Talk with Einstein," *The Listener* 54 (1955): 370–71.

anyone not experiencing the awe of the universe was devoid of a basic human insight.

Yet, having said this, Einstein also insisted that the most profound question one could ask is, "Is the universe friendly?" Einstein, with his magnificent mind, could speak with rapt awe about the mind of God in creation, but he could not answer the question he regarded most profound, because it is not a question that can be answered by math or science. It is interesting to compare Einstein's reference to the "friendliness" of the universe to the question raised by Dinah, the unlettered preacher from the George Eliot novel cited in chapter 1: "What shall we do if God is not our friend?" People at all levels of investigation and learning face the need to come to some judgment about the nature of that power by which we come into existence and live out our days. Is the universe friendly?

> **We find the truth of the relationship in the experience of relating.**

This question about whether the universe supports us or is indifferent or unmindful of our fate is relational in nature. In relational questions we participate in the answer. We confirm the trustworthiness by risking or making ourselves vulnerable to the other and demonstrating that our trust is justified. To refuse to extend trust to another until we know that person to be indisputably trustworthy is to assure that there will merely be an impersonal, formal relationship. In relational knowledge we do not regard the one who is to be known as an object to be analyzed, measured, and controlled. We interact with the other, entrusting ourselves to the other. We find the truth of the relationship in the experience of relating. For example, to enter into friendship or the covenant of marriage requires that we give ourselves to another so we can deeply know who he or she is. Similarly, knowing the disposition of the total universe toward us requires us to risk and participate, so we can confirm that it may be trusted.

We can be moved to awe by reports from physicists and cosmologists about the mind of God and the intellectual ingenuity of the universe. We can be stirred by the "language of God" found in the recent discoveries about the human genome.[3] All this does tell us about the marvelous mind of God. But like Einstein we also want to know about the disposition of this intricately wrought universe toward us: "Is the universe friendly?" In raising this question, we are referring not to the mind of God but to the heart of God. What can we know of the heart of God?

Faith and History

Job acknowledged to his friends that he had no independent place to stand when he stated his case before God. "Look, he passes by me, and I do not see him; / he moves on, but I do not perceive him" (Job 9:11). There was no umpire between him and God "who might lay his hand on us both" (v. 33). Job was driven to the conclusion that applies to all flesh. We do not have a place to stand outside of the flow of events from which we can determine God's intentions for the human family, a very recent arrival on the planet. Human consciousness and subjectivity, we have learned, represent "nature

---

3   This phrase is used as the title of the book by Francis S. Collins, *The Language of God* (see chap. 2, n. 1).

becoming conscious of itself."[4] So far as we know, we are the first of the created order to reflect on origins and destiny and ponder whether or not we matter in the ultimate scheme of things.

{ We stand in, not above, history. }

If we have learned anything from the modern epoch of our history, it is the lesson of relativity. What we can see and know is related to where we stand in the flow of time. There is no point in our lives at which we can leap out of our situation and view the universe from the perspective of eternity. When the Almighty confronted Job in debate, God questioned Job about his standing. On what basis, God asked, did Job object to the direction of events in the world. "Where were you when I laid the foundation of the earth? / Tell me, if you have understanding" (Job 38:4). We each confront our world as a creature within it, not as its creator or judge. What we can know is intimately related to where we stand in the flow of time. As H. Richard Niebuhr reminded us, we are in history as fish are in water.[5]

In the living of our days we observe that certain moments or occasions are particularly transparent and cast meaning on all other events. In our common experience we remember family occasions, anniversaries, career decisions, births, critical illnesses, and a variety of other occurrences that stand out and represent markers in our understanding of who we are.

---

4   Ted Peters in Ted Peters, Robert John Russell, and Michael Welker, eds., *Resurrection: Theological and Scientific Assessments* (Grand Rapids, MI: Wm. B. Eerdmans, 2002), xii.

5   Niebuhr, *The Meaning of Revelation*, 48 (see chap. 5, n. 5).

Beyond our individual and family lives, communities likewise refer to special occasions that help define the group's identity and shape its conduct. National histories are not merely recitals or series of happenings where one event or one historical figure is as significant as any other. Rather, these shared stories refer to personalities or to events that stand out as defining moments in national life and shape national self-understanding and purpose. The mention of George Washington at Valley Forge or Abraham Lincoln at Gettysburg summons forth images that form our understanding of our country and ourselves as a part of it.

Religious communities also receive their cues about the nature of ultimate reality from certain events that are embodied in tradition and Scripture. What is remembered and enshrined in tradition are not merely neutral reports of the kind that would be written for newscasts or newspapers. What is recorded is an illuminating experience that the faithful interpret as a disclosure of a deeper reality at work in their history. Thus, the narration of the escape of the children of Israel from Pharaoh's army in strictly military terms is not in itself a revelation of God. It was an event as witnessed through the eyes of faith that disclosed the fact that God had seen the suffering of the people and delivered them for the journey into the promised land. The event and its interpretation was the bedrock of faith.

As a religious community gathers and embraces a tradition constituted by such special occasions, that tradition becomes the standard and cue by which future experiences are interpreted. In a certain sense these occasions function as a paradigm as vivid as the Copernican model of the earth revolving around the sun, because they become a means of making sense out of history. Traditions are then refined by the community's continuity through time and by their subsequent experience. They abide as living guides for the character of the community and what God intends for them. They help shape the "plausibility system" by which we understand and interpret the world.[6] To convert to a religious tradition is to embrace that tradition's plausibility system as the world in which one lives.

In Christian tradition, we understand that special occasions disclose a relationship with a Supreme Self, God. While studying the physical world, we can dissect and measure the reality that is displayed before us, objects at our disposal. In matters of faith, however, the reality to which we refer is not an object but a subject with whom we may be in relationship.

Jesus and the Heart of God

In Christian faith the life, teachings, death, and resurrection of Jesus constitute *the* special occasions that are at the center of the entire biblical story and disclose the heart of God. John's Gospel holds that "no one has ever seen God." It continues, "It is God the only Son, who is close to the Father's heart, who has made him known" (1:18). In ordinary conversation, we speak of the heart as the core of that person's character and will, the focus of that person's intentions and goals. We come to trust other people's intentions and purposes because of our experiences with them, events in which they disclose the kind of people they are, their hearts.

---

6   Peter L Berger and Thomas Luckmann, *The Social Construction of Reality: A Treatise in the Sociology of Knowledge* (Garden City, NY: Doubleday, 1967), 156.

The testimony of John's Gospel is that Jesus discloses the heart of God. Everyone lives acting on the basis of some supposition, conscious or not, about the character and intention of the Ultimate Reality. One may regard this Reality as loving or grudging, benign or malicious, redeeming or destructive, benevolent or indifferent. John's Gospel proclaims that the nature of God is redeeming love. The late William Sloane Coffin put it tersely in this way: "I think we know far more of God's heart than we do of the mind of God. It's God's heart that Christ on the cross lays bare for the whole world to see. And 'God is love, and those who abide in love abide in God, and God abides in them' (1 John 4:16). . . . Faith is not believing without proof; it is trusting without reservation."[7]

The faith of the first disciples was based on their conviction that God had come near in Jesus Christ. They did not begin with a theory that Jesus was God or "a god." They did not see him as a deity temporarily confined to flesh who walked among them. Rather, they found that Jesus had made it possible for them to talk and be with God in a new way.[8] The creeds and theories that the church subsequently developed were attempts to explain that "here *God*—the ultimate limit of our existence and the ultimate reality with which we have to do—is encountered, not merely [a human being]."[9] The biblical records are clear and consistent in regarding Jesus as fully human. He was not a semidivine entity who only seemed to participate in our humanity. At the same time,

---

7   Coffin, *Credo*, 40 (see chap. 6, n. 1).

8   Rowan Williams, "In the Place of Jesus: Insights from Origen on Prayer," *Christian Century*, August 6, 2014, 20.

9   Gordon D. Kaufman, *Systematic Theology: A Historicist Perspective* (New York: Charles Scribner's Sons, 1968), 183.

through him they experienced God. From the earliest writings of the New Testament, they "could not think or speak of God apart from Christ, or of Christ apart from God."[10]

Witnesses of God's Self-Revelation in Christ

We gain some notion of how thoroughly those early witnesses associated Jesus with God from the earliest writings in the New Testament. The first written sources in our New Testament were penned by Saint Paul, the former Saul, who before his conversion experience persecuted the followers of "the Way" (Acts 9:2). One of the most chilling verses of the New Testament follows the arrest, testimony, and execution of Stephen by stoning. There in Acts 8:1 the author simply reports: "And Saul approved of their killing him."

It is well known that as Paul (then named Saul) was traveling to Damascus with orders in hand to locate, bind, and bring back to Jerusalem those who "belonged to the Way" he was stunned by a bright light. He heard a voice that said, "Saul, Saul, why do you persecute me?" When Saul asked to whom this voice belonged, the voice responded, "I am Jesus, whom you are persecuting" (Acts 9:1-6). We cannot fully comprehend the radical change that took place in the one who went on to become Paul, an apostle of Jesus Christ, as he went about building up congregations instead of destroying them. Followers of the Way were heard to say, when referring to the former Saul, "The one who formerly

---

10 John Macquarrie, *Jesus Christ in Modern Thought* (London: SCM Press, 1990), 377–78.

was persecuting us is now proclaiming the faith he once tried to destroy" (Galatians 1:23).

Paul's writings to the early Christian congregations he formed preceded the earliest of the four Gospels, Mark, by fifteen or twenty years. Paul's conversion is dated at about 34 CE or about three or four years after the crucifixion and resurrection of Jesus. The first of the seven letters that most scholars agree were written by Paul himself,[11] 1 Thessalonians, was written perhaps in 52 CE, and the remaining six letters were written in the following five or six years.

Unlike the Gospel writers who were to follow, Paul, in his writings to the churches, did not give extensive narratives on the life and ministry of Jesus. He believed in the imminent appearance of the Lord in the heavens (Romans 13:11-14; 1 Corinthians 15:23; 1 Thessalonians 2:19; 3:13; 4:16; 5:23), but he was not extensively acquainted with the earthly ministry of Jesus. He was commissioned an apostle in a postresurrection appearance. Yet he was convinced that God's saving purposes had been revealed in Jesus Christ to him. His mission, then, was to serve as an apostle of Jesus Christ and win converts before Jesus reappeared.[12]

About sixteen years after his dramatic vision and conversion on his way to Damascus, Paul came to Corinth and developed a few house churches. In his correspondence with these congregations, he proclaimed his conviction that God's saving purposes were present in Christ: "In Christ God was reconciling the world to himself, not counting their trespasses against them, and

---

11   Romans, 1 Corinthians, 2 Corinthians, Galatians, Philippians, 1 Thessalonians, Philemon.

12   See Osvaldo D. Vena, *Jesus, Disciple of the Kingdom: Mark's Christology for a Community in Crisis* (Eugene, OR: Pickwick, 2014), 22.

entrusting the message of reconciliation to us. So we are ambassadors for Christ, since God is making his appeal through us" (2 Corinthians 5:19-20).

Paul made it clear that in Christ God was reaching out to forgive and redeem.

In the process of writing to his congregations in Corinth, he reminded them of traditions drawn from older sources about Jesus's ministry. He reminded them of the institution of the Lord's Supper, appealing to a tradition apparently shared by many of the churches (1 Corinthians 11:23-26), and he reminded them of the account of Jesus's death for their sins and God's triumph in raising Jesus from the dead (1 Corinthians 15).

It is striking to see in these earliest writings of our New Testament how quickly Jesus's followers identified him with deity. They did not refer to him as a "superman" or as a human transformed in some fashion as a deity. He was not seen as a member of some hierarchy of superhuman beings. The first Christians were also Jewish and as such were committed to belief in one God only. They could not have countenanced the idea of subdeities or divine figures who shared that status with the God of Israel. Jesus was identified as an expression of God in God's own being, a revelation of the saving purposes of the Mighty One that were brought to fulfillment in Jesus. So closely was Jesus identified with God that Paul and other converts from Judaism considered acts of devotion to the risen Christ to be completely compatible with the vigorous monotheism that was a part of their upbringing.[13]

---

13 For this emphasis see Larry W. Hurtado, *Lord Jesus Christ: Devotion to Jesus in Earliest Christianity* (Grand Rapids, MI: Wm. B. Eerdmans, 2003), 49.

Jesus Christ

The terms used to refer to Jesus reveal the clear identification that Paul, a converted Pharisee, made as the significant and determinative disclosure of God's saving purposes among them. In Paul's seven letters, for example, there are 270 uses of the term *Christos*, or Christ.[14] About half of the 531 uses of that title in the New Testament occur in those seven Pauline letters. The title *Christ* is a Greek translation of the Hebrew *messiah*, the "anointed one" whom God had promised to send to save and redeem the people. The fact that the term was used so regularly without resistance or dispute indicates that it was widely considered appropriate as a title for Jesus in the Christian communities. Use of terms such as "in Christ" or "in Christ Jesus" apparently served as common phrases that depicted the Christian life as one in close affiliation with Jesus, as the very name "Christian" implies.

Lord Jesus

A second term used extensively by Paul in his New Testament writings is *kyrios*, or "lord." Paul used that term in reference to Jesus 180 times. That title also had widespread secular usage among Paul's contemporaries. In Roman and Greek circles, it often denoted someone of superior social status. In their societies, for example, the owner of a slave would be termed that slave's "lord." In some provinces of the Roman Empire the title *lord* referred to the emperor. In pagan cults it was used to connote deities, such as the "Lord" Serapis.

---

14 Ibid., 98.

Among this widespread usage of the term, however, "lord" had a much more specific connotation in Jewish religious circles. Devout Jews, reluctant to pronounce the Hebrew name for God, Yahweh, employed Hebrew and Aramaic translations of "Lord" as designations for deity. Greek-speaking Jews also used *kyrios* as a direct reference to God. In the earliest Christian congregations, "Lord" was used to refer to Jesus. In Paul's writings, the apostle referred to Jesus as Lord, but he also used the term when referring to God. The term is used as well for referring to God in Old Testament references.[15]

In Paul's letter to the Corinthian Christians, addressing the issue of food offered to idols, he clearly distinguished between the church's use of "lord" and that of pagan religions. He dismissed the idols as nonentities: "Indeed, even though there may be so-called gods in heaven or on earth—as in fact there are many gods and many lords—yet for us there is one God, the Father, from whom are all things and for whom we exist, and one Lord, Jesus Christ, through whom are all things and through whom we exist" (1 Corinthians 8:5-6). This distinction made it clear in Paul's mind and in the mind of the Christian community who really was Lord. The testimony of faith was that "Jesus is Lord." The clear implication was that if Jesus is Lord, then pagan idols and Roman emperors were not!

Paul's letter to the Philippians is generally dated at about 56 or 57 CE. In that letter, writing about the relationships appropriate in the Christian community, Paul quoted from a hymn that most believe had been in use in the Christian community since the 40s

---

15 Ibid., 108–13.

CE, and as such may lay claim to represent the convictions of followers of the Way at that early date. In this hymn Paul affirmed that Jesus, the risen Christ, has been given the name above every name:

> Let the same mind be in you that was in Christ Jesus,
>> who, though he was in the form of God,
>>> did not regard equality with God
>>> as something to be exploited,
>> but emptied himself,
>>> taking the form of a slave,
>>> being born in human likeness.
>> And being found in human form,
>>> he humbled himself
>>> and became obedient to the point of death—
>>> even death on a cross.
>
> Therefore God also highly exalted him
>> and gave him the name
>> that is above every name,
> so that at the name of Jesus
>> every knee should bend,
>> in heaven and on earth and under the earth,
> and every tongue should confess
>> that Jesus Christ is Lord,
>> to the glory of God the Father. (Philippians 2:5-11)

Continuing Reflection on Who Jesus Is

Two points need to be made. First, it is clear that very early in the Christian community there was an indissoluble connection in the minds of Christians between Jesus and God. They were seen in such undiluted union that those who were committed to belief in only one God were apparently not troubled in the least by acts of "Christ devotion," as scholar Larry Hurtado has written. Their devotion to Jesus Christ was understood not as devotion to an intermediate deity but to God in God's own being. It is "amazing" how quickly the early Christian documents express a comprehensive interpretation of the meaning of Jesus Christ. Hurtado likens the explosive development of these views to the "Big Bang," the fraction of a second in which the basic structure of the universe flashed into being.[16]

The second point is that the early church continued to grow in their understanding of who Jesus was. Beginning with this fundamental identification of Jesus as God's self-revelation, the first Christians refined their understanding of the meaning of Jesus in keeping with external events, as well as their own deepening discernment of Christ's meaning for them. Their understanding of Jesus grew in decisive steps. For one thing, external events materially changed and affected what it meant to be a follower of Christ. In Paul's earliest writings, the apostolic mission did not involve a concentration on the historical events in Jesus's ministry and the content of his teachings. The point was the lordship of Jesus Christ, his sacrificial death and resurrection, and the coming

---

16 Ibid., 135.

close of history that Paul believed to be at hand. As an apostle it was his mission to proclaim Jesus Christ as glorified Lord and to save sinners from hell and prepare them for the glorious future assured by Christ, soon to be revealed.[17]

Accordingly, there is a change in the terms used for Christians and for Christ. Paul, for example, did not use the term *disciple*. He referred to Christians as "believers" and to himself as an "apostle." The word *disciple* is used solely in the four Gospels and in Acts. By tradition, Paul died in Rome in the mid-60s, perhaps 66, according to Ignatius of Antioch. The Gospel of Mark was written after Paul's death, and it reflected the reality of the Jewish–Roman wars and the destruction of the temple in Jerusalem in 70 CE. For those in the Christian faith community in those years, it was painfully clear that the Lord had not returned and that the task of his followers was to duplicate the pattern of his life. That is what it meant to be a disciple.[18]

Christ

Even the term *Christos* (Greek for "messiah"), or "Christ," so commonly used in the first decades as to be almost a proper name for Jesus, was not widely applied to Jesus at the outset. Some question whether Jesus accepted the title of "Messiah" in his lifetime. As the use of "Christ" grew, its meaning had to be revised in keeping with understandings of the death and resurrection of Jesus. Far from representing the conquering military figure, Jesus

---

17 Vena, *Jesus, Disciple of the Kingdom.*

18 This is the interpretation outlined by, among others, Vena in *Jesus, Disciple of the Kingdom.*

suffered death and humiliation and was raised from the dead. So, the term *Christ*, whenever it was used, was redefined and transformed in a manner that was appropriate for the suffering servant, whose life, death, and exultation represented healing and pardon from sin.[19]

Son of Man

A similar growth in insight can be observed in the extensive use of "Son of Man" as a title for Jesus. Contemporary scholars are quite confident that the term so often used later in the Gospels as a title for Jesus was originally used to mean a human being. Some conclude that Jesus used the term primarily in the conventional sense of referring to a person.[20] As the early Christians reflected on the meaning of Jesus, it was natural to associate him with the figure referred to in Daniel 7:13. In the Jerusalem Bible this verse, depicting Daniel's dream, reads: "I gazed into the visions of the night, / And I saw, coming on the clouds of heaven, / one like a son of man." The New Standard Revised Version translates it: "As I watched in the night visions, / I saw one like a human being / coming with the clouds of heaven." The figure here represents not merely a human being but a heavenly figure who was given dominion and glory. Even if, as some insist, Jesus did not apply the term to himself, it quickly became a term to express the glory of the risen Christ, who sits at the right hand of God.

----

19 Macquarrie, *Jesus Christ in Modern Thought*, 38–39.
20 See, for example, John Dominic Crossan, *The Historical Jesus: The Life of a Mediterranean Jewish Peasant* (San Francisco: HarperCollins, 1991), 241–43.

Logos

Perhaps the continuing refinement of Christian views of Jesus Christ is nowhere more evident than in the Gospel of John. This Gospel is considered the latest of the four Gospels and is dated in the period 90–110 CE.[21] In this Gospel, in contrast to the first three, Jesus is described as the Word (*logos*) made flesh (1:1, 14). In Greek philosophical thought the Word is the logic or intention of God by which God made all that is. The Gospel of John pictures Jesus as coexistent with God: "If you knew me," Jesus said, "you would know my Father also" (8:19). "Whoever sees me sees him who sent me," he said elsewhere (12:45). Extensive passages in John's Gospel deal with the "I am" sayings, words attributed to Jesus that deal with his distinctive person and mission.

The use of philosophical concepts such as the *logos* reflects the attempt to interpret the meaning of Jesus Christ in terms that were in use at the time the Gospel was written. Even if it is granted that many of these philosophical concepts were already a part of Palestinian Judaism at the time of the writing of the Gospel of John,[22] the prominence of these concepts, ones not present in the first three Gospels, shows the early Christians' efforts to interpret their faith in terms meaningful to their culture. A similar effort is a necessary part of witnessing to Christ in each generation. However, the central conviction of these earliest witnesses continues to be a witness of the contemporary church. Our conviction is

---

21 D. Moody Smith, *John*, Abingdon New Testament Commentaries (Nashville: Abingdon Press, 1999), 43.

22 As contended by Raymond E. Brown, The Anchor Bible: *The Gospel According to John (I-XII)* (Garden City, NY: Doubleday & Company, Inc., 1966), LXIV.

that in Christ we are brought near to God in saving faith. "In Christ God was reconciling the world to himself" (2 Corinthians 5:19).

Son of God

The title "Son of God" was employed in the New Testament to express the meaning of Christ. In the Old Testament the title was variously used to designate a heavenly being, Israel's earthly king, or Israel itself. While New Testament writers occasionally refer to believers as "children of God" (Matthew 5:9) or "children of the Most High" (Luke 6:35), the primary usage of the term "Son of God" is directed to Jesus. For example, in The Gospel According to Mark, Jesus was referred to as God's Son twice by voices from heaven (at the baptism, 1:11; at the transfiguration, 9:7; and finally by the centurion at the crucifixion, 15:39). In response to the high priest's question, Jesus accepted this title, and then promptly identified himself with the title "Son of Man" (14:62).

Mark's, the earliest Gospel's, reference to Jesus as the "Son of God" continues and in some sense is intensified in the following three Gospels and Paul's writings. In the opening of Paul's letter to the Romans, there is a reference to what is regarded as a very early tradition in the church. Using this tradition, Paul referred at the outset of the letter to Jesus as "descended from David according to the flesh and . . . declared to be Son of God with power according to the spirit of holiness by resurrection from the dead" (1:3-4). Jesus's frequent reference to his relationship with God in close personal terms, referring to God by the familiar Aramaic intimate term for the male parent, *abba*, doubtless fortified the early church's tendency to speak of Jesus as "Son of God." The term continues to serve well to express the identification and close connection between Jesus Christ and God. The language of sonship serves to indicate the intimate connection of Jesus with God and how he represents God's power and presence with us.

Word

We have already referred to metaphors of "the Word" also employed by John's Gospel. Though it originated from philosophical concepts that had been embraced by elements of Judaism, it served to express the manner in which Jesus embodied God's purpose and intention, God's plan and vision for life.

Other Metaphors

Some later metaphors in subsequent centuries sought to interpret in terms congenial with the church's surroundings how Christians understood the relationship of Jesus Christ to God. Their efforts in part were prompted by their intent to represent the faith to the educated people in the Mediterranean with whom they interacted. In that area the teachings of Platonism and Stoicism attracted significant attention. Apologists for Christian faith were led to employ philosophical terms then in use to explain the meaning of Christ for their contemporary audience. For example, the Council of Nicea (325 CE) employed language of being to declare that Christ is of one substance (*homoousios*) with God the Father. It remained for the Council of Chalcedon (451 CE) to declare that the two natures, human and divine, in Christ are present "without confusion, without change, without division, without separation."[23] This

---

23 Quoted in Macquarrie, *Jesus Christ in Modern Thought*, 165.

classic expression determined that Christ is known in the church to be fully human and fully divine.

We falter in interpreting the faith whenever, for example, we fail to insist on the full humanity and the full divinity of Jesus. Here is how one recent interpreter phrased the conclusion of Chalcedon that Jesus is fully human and fully divine: "Jesus is both a mirror to our humanity and a window to divinity, a window revealing as much of God as is given mortal eyes to see. When Christians see Christ empowering the weak, scorning the powerful, healing the wounded, and judging their tormentors, we are seeing transparently the power of God at work. What is finally important is not that Christ is Godlike, but that God is Christ-like."[24]

Another recent interpreter attempts to express the conclusions of ancient councils in more contemporary terms. Speaking of Jesus Christ, Maurice Wiles wrote:

> He was not just one who had taught about God; he was not just one who had lived a life of perfect human response to God. He had lived a life that embodied and expressed God's character and action in the world. As prophets in the past had expressed the word of God that had come to them not only in speech but in symbolic action, so in a far more comprehensive way did Jesus. The impact not merely of his teaching but of his whole person communicated the presence and the power of God with an unprecedented sense of directness and finality.[25]

---

24 Coffin, *Credo*, 12 (see chap. 6, n. 1).
25 Maurice Wiles, *Explorations in Christology* (N.p.: SCM Press, 1979), 24, quoted in Macquarrie, *Jesus Christ in Modern Thought*, 8.

These expressions, and many others that might be added, illustrate the continuing effort of Christians to express the faith in terms that are consistent with the founding insights of the Christian community and that communicate with today's world. They remind us that in Christian faith we cannot think of God in terms other than those we find in Jesus Christ. We refer to him not merely as a compilation of his teachings, central though the teachings are, but to his life, the community founded following his resurrection, and the continuing insights and interpretation of the community guided by the Holy Spirit. When we speak of knowing God in Jesus Christ, therefore, we are speaking of the whole event of Jesus—his life, teachings, death and resurrection, and the community formed to interpret and follow his message.

Even this brief glance at some of the more formal efforts to interpret and clarify the relationship between Jesus and God illustrates that professing Christian faith requires a continuing dialogue between our faith in Christ and terms that convey meaning to our present context. Some of the terms employed in ancient controversies do not connect with our ways of thinking today. For example, we are not likely to think of the person of Jesus in terms of his "substance" and the relationship of that substance with the substance of God. But these conclusions, even if phrased in unfamiliar terms, do convey boundary markers in the ways that the church still refers to God and to Christ.

Jesus, God Made Known

As we have seen, the earliest witnesses found that in relating to Jesus they were led to God. While they were devoted to worship of only one God, they saw no conflict between that commitment and acts of "Christ devotion." We have noted that Jesus Christ was not understood as a competing deity but as an expression of God. The first Christians were assured that God was Christlike, that there was a direct correlation between the presence of Christ in their midst and the heart of God.

John's Gospel incorporates this belief in its report of Jesus's word to Thomas: "If you know me, you will know my Father also" (14:7). The use of *logos* or *Word* in John's prologue (1:1-18) makes the witness clear. Jesus is depicted as he who represents the inner thought and intentions of God. For John, to see Jesus is to see God.

Jesus's Actions

The nature and intent of God are disclosed in several dimensions of Jesus's ministry. Jesus's actions, for example, disclose that God seeks out the lost. Jesus associated with people who were written off as sinners, and thereby as people who had no standing before God. Jesus kept company with them and was condemned by the Pharisees for doing so. The Pharisees were devout Jews with whom Jesus otherwise shared many beliefs. For example, unlike the Sadducees, both Jesus and the Pharisees believed in the resurrection of the dead. Jesus befriended the Pharisees and enjoyed being a guest in their homes. Despite their friendship with Jesus, many of the Pharisees decried his association with sinners. They viewed this as an erosion of standards and as a violation of their notion of God's righteousness. Jesus insisted that there was joy in heaven over the return of the lost. The parables of the joy that was appropriate at the recovery of the lost (in Luke 15) were spoken to respond to the Pharisees' criticism. The gathering of those dismissed as sinners in Jesus's mind was a sign of the coming of the kingdom of God, not an indication of its demise. In Jesus's actions and in his parables, his characteristic way of speaking, God is shown to seek reunion with those regarded as the lost and to offer forgiveness out of sheer grace.

Jesus interpreted the return of the disinherited of the religious establishment as a sure sign of God's grace and forgiveness. God's outgoing grace was seen in the joy of the prodigal's father, who surrendered his dignity in order to meet the returning son on the road and restore his standing in the family before the son could even ask for acceptance. Jesus attributed God's forgiveness to the sheer graciousness of God's nature. He portrayed God's readiness to forgive in the landowner's retort to those who objected to his granting of a full day's salary for an hour's labor in the cool of the day: "Am I not allowed to do what I choose with what belongs to me? Or are you envious because I am generous?" (Matthew 20:15).

God's healing purposes are shown as well as Jesus reaches out to those broken in body or spirit. When John's disciples inquired about his ministry, Jesus reported the results: "The blind receive their sight, the lame walk, the lepers are cleansed, the deaf hear, the dead are raised, the poor have good news brought to them" (Luke 7:22). The people who were thought to be outside the circle of God's favor were the ones who were made whole. The poor, who then were presumed to be scorned by God for some failing of their own, heard good news instead of rejection and blame.

Jesus and the Kingdom of God

Jesus's actions disclosed that it was the nature of God to forgive and reclaim. Jesus called disciples to join him in seeing what God was doing. His actions fit into an inclusive vision of God's readiness to bring in the kingdom of God or the reign of God.

The kingdom of God as Jesus presented it was not a static entity. It represented the shape of relationships when God's righteous will is present and heeded in daily affairs. In Jesus's teaching the kingdom of God is both a present force and a future expectation. Men and women see the kingdom when God restores them to health and when God overcomes their alienation and restores a right relationship with them. The kingdom of God contrasts with the realms of the demonic and oppressive. The kingdom is present when the demonic forces that twist and distort human life are overcome and men and women are free to live as God intends.

The gospel in the first instance does not prescribe something we are to believe or to do. Rather, it commends a certain way of looking at the world. Jesus proclaimed that the kingdom or reign of God was breaking in. The Beatitudes, for example (Matthew 5:1-11; Luke 6:20-22) were not rules to follow but were ways of seeing what the world looked like in the light of the kingdom of God. The blessed of God were not the powerful and the officially pious. They were the poor, the hungry, and those who wept. Their consolation was at hand. See the world, we are urged, from the perspective of those who are usually regarded as losers and written off, for they are the ones who are blessed by

God and destined to inherit the earth. They are the very children of God.[26]

Jesus did not deliver his message in propositions to which he asked people to give their assent. He told stories, parables, about what the world looks like when the kingdom of God comes. Over half of Jesus's teaching in Luke's Gospel, for example, is given in the form of parables; in Matthew's Gospel 43 percent, and about 12 percent in the Gospel of Mark. The stories are not necessarily about explicitly religious subjects either. Only one or possibly two of the forty-six parables told by Jesus in the first three Gospels deals with religious subjects.[27] His stories are about a forgiving father and a rebellious son, a gracious farmer who pays a full day's wage to those who had worked only an hour, and a wedding banquet to which the street people are invited. All of these settings are taken out of common life and employed to provide a glimpse of God's coming reign.

Access to God through Jesus

The first followers of Jesus also found a new way of speaking with God. Jesus spoke with God on intimate terms as his Father. He at times employed the intimate term *abba* (daddy), to convey his relationship. New believers found that they themselves could refer to God in this manner: "God has sent the Spirit of his Son into our hearts," said Saint Paul, "crying, 'Abba! Father!'" (Galatians 4:6). When Jesus was sorely tested between obedience to God

---

26 This interpretation was offered by Stanley Hauerwas and William H. Willimon in their *Resident Aliens* (Nashville: Abingdon Press, 1989), 88.

27 See Neal F. Fisher, *The Parables of Jesus: Glimpses of God's Reign,* rev. ed. (New York: Crossroad, 1990), chap. 2.

and his natural desire to be delivered, he prayed, "Abba, Father . . . remove this cup from me; yet, not what I want, but what you want" (Mark 14:36).

In helping his disciples reach out for God, he employed the liturgy of the synagogue. He clearly followed the Aramaic Kaddish prayer that Jews like himself prayed in the synagogue. It read, "Magnified and sanctified be his great name in the world which he has created according to his will. May he establish his kingdom in your lifetime and in your days and in the lifetime of all the house of Israel even speedily and at a near time."[28] It is evident that this prayer, still in use in modern times, helped shape Jesus's model prayer. Addressed to "our Father," the prayer asks for God's righteous rule to shape the affairs of our world and for God's kingdom to reign in our world, even as it does in heaven.

In instructing us to pray to "our Father," Jesus gives us confidence in approaching God in our prayer. "We begin," says Rowan Williams, "by expressing the confidence that we stand where Jesus stands and can say what Jesus says."[29] In effect Jesus prays with us when we pray in his name. It is *our* Father to whom we are authorized to speak with the assurance that it is God's will to give us what we really need.

In his parable of the friend at midnight (Luke 11:5-8), Jesus depicted a situation that would have been familiar to his hearers.[30] A householder goes to a friend and asks for bread to share with another friend who has arrived at his door at midnight. It would be

---

28 Translation by G. Dalman, quoted in Norman Perrin, *Rediscovering the Teaching of Jesus* (New York: Harper & Row, 1967), 57.
29 Williams, "In the Place of Jesus," 20.
30 See Fisher, *The Parables of Jesus*, 116ff.

understood that the friend had traveled at night to avoid the heat of the day. Even if his friend is personally reluctant to respond, it is unthinkable, in Jesus's telling, that he would decline to help a neighbor in need. Even if the friend is not generous, social pressure alone would assure that he would get out of bed and come forth with the bread. He would have offended the whole community had he declined this clear obligation of hospitality. The community's honor was involved in extending hospitality. A negative response was unthinkable. So, asks Jesus, how much more will God, who is gracious and generous, be prepared to give you what you ask in prayer? The conclusion, then, is clear: "So I say to you, Ask, and it will be given you; search, and you will find; knock, and the door will be opened for you. For everyone who asks receives, and everyone who searches finds, and for everyone who knocks, the door will be opened" (vv. 9-10).

Jesus's Suffering and Vindication

Jesus's disclosure of the character of God to the eyes of faith is nowhere more evident than in his violent death and resurrection. In obedience to God, Jesus accepted the humiliation and pain of the cross, even praying to God for those who reviled him to be forgiven (Luke 23:34). There, says Jürgen Moltmann, we see God experiencing abandonment and suffering for the sake of human sin. "God died on the cross of Christ, says Christian faith so that we might live and rise again in his future."[31] Here in the face of human depravity and sin we see the clear picture

---

31 Jürgen Moltmann, *The Crucified God,* trans. R. A. Wilson and John Bowden (New York: Harper & Row, 1974), 216.

of God's nature. God in Christ experiences abandonment and humiliation and discloses the divine love that forgives, heals, and redeems.

The proclamation of Easter is the story of God's victory over sin and death by raising Jesus from the dead. The disciples witnessed the worst. The one in whom they trusted underwent public humiliation, scorn, and excruciating pain and death. Their hopes were crushed. "We had hoped that he was the one to redeem Israel," some of them lamented to the unknown traveler who joined them as they trudged to Emmaus (Luke 24:21). And as they broke bread, they recognized that it was the Lord. When they reported the marvelous news to the disciples meeting together back in Jerusalem, the Lord appeared to them as well (v. 36). Indeed, in the earliest written account of Jesus's resurrection, Paul referred to a yet earlier tradition of Jesus's appearances to more than five hundred of the brothers and sisters, most of whom were still alive, and at last to him (1 Corinthians 15:6-9).

The testimony of Paul and the earlier tradition upon which he drew is that God shows God's heart in offering redemptive love. The heart of God is laid bare on the cross for all to see. God is love. God seeks out the lost and suffers for the redemption of all. The suffering and humiliation formed in sin is overcome in that love. The resurrection discloses that in the end God triumphs over the worst of human sin. And God is "all in all" (1 Corinthians 15:28).

{ Jesus is God's parable. }

Trusting Jesus and Knowing God

While no one has seen God, we affirm with John's Gospel that the Son who is near the heart of God made God known (1:18). We might refer to Jesus as a parable of God. The parable discloses the ultimate amid the immediate. Jesus, always proclaimed as completely human, also represents the intentions and the heart of God. Just as the parables provide for us a glimpse of a reality beyond their immediate particular reference, so a specific life, death, and resurrection point to a reality that is beyond the concrete circumstances of his ministry. The church's faithful witness has consistently been that Jesus is fully human, fully divine.

> { Jesus and we are in it together. }

It is essential to continue expressing in concepts, analogies, and metaphors how Jesus represents God to us, but these remain human efforts to respond to a divine initiative and are not themselves objects of devotion. Our loyalty as Christians is to Jesus Christ and not to the theories, assumptions, or beliefs by which we seek to understand him. Albert Schweitzer, medical missionary and New Testament scholar, arrived at the same conclusion in his well-known writing early in the last century, *The Quest for the Historical Jesus.* In the concluding sentences of the book, he wrote: "The names in which men [and women] expressed their recognition of Him as such, Messiah, Son of Man, Son of God, have become for us historical parables. We can find no designation which expresses what he is for us." Then he concluded with these famous lines:

He comes to us as One unknown, without a name, as of old,
by the lake side, he came to those men who knew Him not. He
speaks to us the same word: "Follow thou me!" and sets us to
the tasks which He has to fulfill in our time. He commands.
And to those who obey, whether they be wise or simple, He will
reveal Himself in the toils, the conflicts, the sufferings which
they shall pass through in his fellowship, and, as an ineffable
mystery, they shall learn in their own experience Who He is.[32]

The man or woman who embraces the gospel stands with
Jesus in acknowledging a God whose name and nature is love. We
trust that God is Christlike, that what we have seen in Christ is the
heart of God. To accept Christ is to fuse the story of one's life with
the story of Christ. It is to see the world through the perspective
of the Gospel account. It is to stand with Jesus in trusting God and
placing our lives in God's hands. "To become a Christian involves
learning the story of Israel and of Jesus well enough to interpret
and experience oneself and one's world in its terms.[33] Such faith
enabled the apostle Paul to write to the people in Galatia, "I have
been crucified with Christ; and it is no longer I who live, but it is
Christ who lives in me. And the life I now live in the flesh I live by
faith in the Son of God" (Galatians 2:19-20).

Christian theologian W. Paul Jones expresses this fundamental trust in striking terms:

Rejected, betrayed, and deserted, Jesus expresses final
words of trust: "Into your hands . . ." If it were not for Jesus,

---

32 Quoted in Crossan, *The Historical Jesus,* 225.
33 Lindbeck, *The Nature of Doctrine,* 34 (see chap. 4, n. 11).

I would be an atheist. I cannot do what he did. Immersed in a world filled with suffering and death, I cannot trust what he trusted. Jesus's final words represent the chasm I cannot bridge. On my own, I cannot leap from *why* to *into.* I cannot. This is why I am a Christian. Faith means trust the Jesus who was able to trust God as Father. Jesus and I are in it together.[34]

Trusting Jesus is to receive him as God made known and to join him in placing our trust in God. Jesus and we are in it together.

REFLECTION QUESTIONS

1. What five or six events in your life are most helpful in summing up who you are as a person and what is most meaningful to you?

2. Do you agree that we all have some assumptions—acknowledged or not—about the character of the world around us? Have you known any who regarded the world as meaningless, malicious, and menacing? How has this affected their actions?

3. Do you find it difficult to think of Jesus as both fully human and fully divine? Do you tend to focus on one more than the other? What benefit is there in holding the two together?

4. What does it mean, as William Sloane Coffin affirms, to refer to Jesus as "both a mirror to our humanity and a

---

34 W. Paul Jones, *Becoming Who God Wants You to Be: 60 Meditations for Personal Spiritual Direction* (Nashville: Upper Room Books, 2013), 74.

window to divinity, a window revealing as much of God as is given mortal eyes to see"?

5. In this chapter there are four illustrations of the way Jesus makes God known: his actions and teachings in his ministry, his embodiment of the kingdom of God, his access to God, and his suffering and vindication. Which of these are most helpful to you in understanding who God is?

6. What does it mean to you to refer to Jesus as a parable of God?

7. What question(s) would you address to the theologian W. Paul Jones in response to his statement at the end of this chapter?

Chapter 7

Faith Seeking Understanding

I commit myself in order that I may understand.
—Anselm, Archbishop of Canterbury
(1033?–1109)[1]

Always have your answer ready for people who ask you the reason for the hope that you all have. But give it with courtesy and respect.

—1 Peter 3:15-16 (Jerusalem Bible)

The late John Updike attended church and was well-schooled in Christian theology. He was a believer, but like many believers, he occasionally raised critical questions about the content of that belief. In one of his short stories, he wrote of churchgoing as an

---

1   This translation is by Karen Armstrong in her *The Case for God*, 132 (see chap. 4, n. 2). The phrase from Anselm is traditionally translated "I believe in order that I may understand." Armstrong reminds us that the word "believe" as originally used meant not assent to a doctrine but a commitment of the heart. Her new translation seeks to restore that meaning to Anselm's statement.

opportunity "to sit and stand in unison and sing and recite creeds and petitions that are like paths worn smooth in the raw terrain of our hearts." In church, he said, he listened as a preacher "strives to console us with scraps of ancient epistles and halting accounts, hopelessly compromised by words, of those intimations of divine joy that are like pain in that, their instant gone, the mind cannot remember or believe them."[2]

Updike is not the only vigilant believer to report moments of dissonance between what he believed from the bottom of his heart and what he could comprehend off the top of his mind. Faith's "intimations of divine joy" sometimes flee both memory and belief. Even the sturdiest believer will at times encounter troubling doubt.

Perhaps few, if any, were more ardent or effective voices for faith in the twentieth century than the Oxford professor C. S. Lewis. Yet even this prolific author and defender of the faith spoke candidly of his brushes with doubt. In a letter to a friend, Lewis wrote:

> I think the trouble with me is *lack of faith*. I have no rational ground for going back on the arguments that convinced me of God's existence: but the irrational deadweight of my old skeptical habits, and the spirit of this age, and the cares of the day, steal away all my lively feeling of the truth, and often when I pray I wonder if I am not posting letters to a non-existent address. Mind you I don't *think* so—the whole of my reasonable mind is convinced: but I often *feel* so.[3]

---

2   John Updike, "Packed Dirt, Churchgoing, a Dying Cat, a Traded Car," in *Pigeon Feathers and Other Stories* (New York: Alfred A. Knopf, 1962).

3   Quoted in McGrath, *Doubting*, 9 (see chap. 3, n. 2).

Even the devoted Saint Teresa of Calcutta, lauded around the world for her devotion to the dying poor in Calcutta, confessed in her letters that at times in her life she had troubling and recurring doubts about the existence of God.[4]

When we recognize that even vigilant believers experience moments or seasons of doubt, it is well to remind ourselves that beliefs may change while faith endures. Faith remains as a commitment to live on the conviction that certain things are true. But the ways that we phrase those truths and how we confirm them may undergo revision and change. Dr. Harry Emerson Fosdick, founding pastor of Riverside Church in New York City, used to say that astronomy changes but the stars abide.

The life of any vigilant believer will likely include moments when he or she seeks to understand how one's faith squares with all that we know about the world through other means. Faith seeks understanding and struggles with doubt.

Struggles with Doubt

People of faith are called to remember that faith is a matter of trust and commitment and not merely acceptance of propositions about God. Faith is capable of guiding us even if we are uncertain about the precise way to express it. In faith, vigilant believers are relieved of the illusion, as physicist and theologian Ian Barbour puts it, "of having put God in a creed." Faith "permits us to live and act amid the uncertainties of life without pretensions of intellectual

---

4 *New York Times* reports on Saint Teresa's collection of letters, *Come Be My Light*, cited in Cox, *The Future of Faith*, 17 (see chap. 4, n. 8).

or moral infallibility."[5] But seasons of doubt do prompt us to seek further understanding.

{ Faith guides us during times of uncertainty. }

Fideism

To be sure, there are ways that some believers seek to avoid any challenge from doubt. Some avoid conflict by clinging rigorously to certain interpretations of sacred Scripture, certain creeds or doctrine. For them these authorities are to be clung to no matter how they conflict with what is known from other sources. Findings of the physical sciences, for example, are automatically dismissed by these believers if those findings appear to conflict with the words of Scripture or tradition. This "fideism," as it is called, requires that one screen out information about the world and create faith as a citadel of belief protected from any challenge. The life of faith for such individuals must be a defensive effort. Despite the believer's intent, faith may cease to be a living relationship with God and become instead a devotion to propositions and doctrines about God.

The Religious Fictionalist

Another stance that avoids the search of faith for understanding heads in quite a different direction. In this response individuals maintain the outward appearance of faith solely for the incentive and support it provides for the moral life. Intellectually these

---

5   Ian G. Barbour, *Myths, Models and Paradigms* (New York: Harper & Row, 1974), 137.

individuals are actually atheists with their minds. They nonetheless consider the "illusion" of belief to be conducive to good morals and conduct. They hold that the stance and language of belief help them remain true to their moral convictions even if they believe that they are strictly human preferences that lack any grounding in a deeper reality. One such person described herself this way: "I am a religious fictionalist. I don't just banish all religious sentences to the flames. I make believe some of them are true, and I think that's all to the good."[6]

> { Doubt can prompt us to seek deeper understanding. }

Philosopher Richard Braithwaite expressed a similar view of religious language when he described affirmations of faith merely as statements of intent to act in a certain way. He continued, "It is not necessary, in my view, for the asserter of a religious assertion to believe in the truth of the story involved in the assertions: what is necessary is that the story should be entertained in thought . . . Many people find it easier to resolve upon and to carry through a cause of action which is contrary to their natural inclinations if this policy is associated in their minds with certain stories."[7]

It is clear that neither the adherent to fideism nor the self-described "religious fictionalist" will have a reason to struggle for understanding of his or her faith. For the fideist, there is no *cause*

---

6   Jean Kazez, quoted in William Irwin, "How to Live a Lie," *Opinionator* (blog), November 2, 2015, https://opinionator.blogs.nytimes.com/2015/11/02/how -to-live-a-lie/?_r=0.

7   Richard Braithwaite, *An Empiricist's View of the Nature of Religious Belief* (London and New York: Cambridge University Press, 1955), 26–27.

to relate faith to knowledge of the world since faith occupies a privileged and unassailable position. The religious fictionalist, on the other hand, has made the prior judgment that there is no reality to which the language of faith refers, so she has already decided that there is no *possibility* of grounding the language of morals and truth in a deeper realm.

Conviction of Things Not Seen

If we are people of faith, however, we do have a need to reconcile the reality we grasp—or that grasps us—with all that we know through other means. Astronomer Robert Jastrow, writing about faith, put it bluntly: "We cannot believe what we do not think is true."[8] People of faith hold to the conviction that the world and the processes by which it evolves are the expression of God. For them, trust in God, the Last Reality, leads them to comprehend the world more fully and to live a more fulfilling life. They expect that they will find expressions of the divine mind within the created order. In short, people of faith should expect to find correlation or consonance between faith in God and the world God has created. We cannot commend a moral ideal or pattern of life unless we hold a conviction that this is the kind of world in which such is appropriate. We naturally believe that our faith will help us understand the world and that the world will shed light on the fundamental reality of God.

Unless, therefore, we are fideists, who see no need to seek further understanding, or fictionalists, who sense no possibility of

---

8   Robert Jastrow, *God and the Astronomers*, 2nd ed. (New York: W. W. Norton, 1992), 118.

relating the contents of faith to the real world, we as people of faith need to seek understanding, so in that process it is natural to experience a struggle with doubt.

The Dimensions of Doubt

We can compare doubt to the way an otherwise healthy body deals with disease. One medical practitioner suggested that life is an ongoing struggle against disease. Health is a condition in which the body successfully resists disease and functions effectively.[9] It is possible to think of doubt as the natural and healthy effort of the mind and spirit to comprehend what appears to be a contradiction between what is believed and what is observed. Faith as it seeks understanding strives to correlate the insights of faith and to utilize them in understanding the world more fully.

To experience periodic doubt is not the same as a permanent state of skepticism. Skepticism, however, is also a kind of faith in that it is the conviction, incapable of proof, that nothing about ultimate reality is knowable by humans. Similarly, periodic doubt is not the same as unbelief or atheism. Atheists believe that they can discern the final reality that surrounds us and thereby reach the conclusion that there is no God and that the natural world and its processes are the only realities in our world. This is not the absence of faith; rather it is the expression of an alternative faith. It is a faith because it is an outlook on the world that is neither provable nor measurable.

---

9   Illustration from McGrath, *Doubting*, 14.

Faith as it seeks understanding should be viewed in relational terms. In any relationship there is a need to reach out with a commitment, which outruns our capacity to understand. When we establish a friendship we have some evidence about the one we are befriending. Yet we do not withhold any relationship with the friend until we have investigated everything about her. Even on the human level there will inevitably be elements in that person's psyche that we will not know or understand. Friendship is committing ourselves in trust to others in order to know who they are. In the context of this commitment, whether as a casual friend, a longtime friend, or even a marriage partner, we discover and comprehend more fully the depths of another person.

> To experience periodic doubt is not the same as a permanent state of skepticism.

If this is true in human relationships, how much more must it be true in our relationship with the Last Reality before whom we live? The person of faith, in seeking understanding, commits to trust in God. In living out this trust and commitment, we learn more fully the nature of God. "Faith," said William Sloane Coffin, "must be lived before it is understood, and the more it is lived, the more things become possible." Faith, he added, is not a substitute for thought. "Faith, in fact, is what makes good thinking possible."[10]

Human Finitude and Limitation

To say that we learn more fully, however, does not mean that we with our limited minds and spirits can fully discern the nature of God

---

10 Coffin, *Credo*, 10, 141 (see chap. 6, n. 1).

or the purpose of all that we encounter. What we experience as doubt is in part the experience of our thoughts running up hard against the limits of our minds. Albert Einstein, in a 1932 letter to Queen Elizabeth of Belgium, commented, "As a human being one has been endowed with intelligence to be able to see clearly how utterly inadequate that intelligence is when confronted with what exists."[11]

When we reduce the mystery of our existence to the confines of our minds, we need to remind ourselves that we humans are last-minute arrivals on a planet circling one of countless billions of stars. By some mysterious process, the elements that formed our bodies sprang to life and consciousness. Mindful of our origins, we should not be surprised that our minds fail fully to understand the massive mind and universe that brought us forth. Indeed, any God who could be comprehended by our human minds would not be God but a human approximation of God. It would represent an idol; that is, an object of our own making to which we give our souls' praise. The prophet Isaiah reminds us of the contrast between our capacities and the sway of the Mighty One:

> Have you not known? Have you not heard?
>> Has it not been told you from the beginning? . . .
> It is he who sits above the circle of the earth,
>> and its inhabitants are like grasshoppers;
> who stretches out the heavens like a curtain,
>> and spreads them like a tent to live in;
> who brings princes to naught,
>> and makes the rulers of the earth as nothing.
> (Isaiah 40:21-23)

---

11   Quoted in McGrath, *Doubting*, 22.

The frailty of our minds and spirits may keep us from understanding the astounding affirmation that God, who is the one before whom we humans are as grasshoppers, also is the One who cares for us: "Cast all your anxiety on him, because he cares for you" (1 Peter 5:7). Because our own capacities are limited, we may well have moments when it is impossible for us to conceive that the Holy One who sits above the circle of the earth even knows, much less cares, about us. We should remind ourselves that our incapacity to imagine a reality does not mean that the reality is not there.

We should remember that even in the sciences, seemingly the model of precision and certainty, researchers must speak of realities that have never been and never could be observed. Particle physicists, for example, deal with phenomena that cannot be imagined, let alone measured and observed. For example, John Polkinghorne, a physicist and theologian, reported, "No one has ever seen a quark, and we believe that no one ever will." Yet he affirms that their existence is necessary because they help make sense of a lot of laboratory results he has experienced.[12] If the "hard sciences" must believe in realities that are beyond observation and imagination, we should not be surprised that the compassion and care of the Almighty at times exceed our capacity to imagine or think. Some doubts may simply be a reflection of the limits of our minds and imaginations.

Patterns of Living

It is also possible that one of the dimensions of doubt arises out of a pattern of living. In the context of modern science it has been said

---

12 Polkinghorne, *Quarks,* 116 (see chap. 2, n. 14).

that we do not see the world as *it is* but rather as *we are*. The Bible rarely even troubles to speak on behalf of the existence of God. On one of those few occasions when the subject is broached, Psalm 14:1 (parallel in Psalm 53:1), doubters are dismissed as "fools." We quickly note, however, that the basis of their doubt is not intellectual. Their doubt is based on a pattern of living that does not acknowledge God's reality. Those who are termed "fools" are the assertive, autonomous "go-getters" whom our society often lauds and rewards. Here they are dismissed as fools because of their "practical atheism," their ordering of their lives as if God is not there. It turns out that their practical exclusion of God from their lives is not a product of their thinking. Rather, it is an outcome issuing from the way they treat their fellow human beings. "They have all gone astray, they are all alike perverse. . . . / Have they no knowledge, all the evildoers / who eat up my people as they eat bread, / and do not call upon the LORD?" (Psalm 14:3-4).

We recall that C. S. Lewis, in discussing his moments of doubt, referred to the "old skeptical habits, and the spirit of this age, and the cares of the day" that "steal away my lively feeling of the truth." This in turn led him in moments of doubt to think that his prayers were directed to a "non-existent address." It is well for us to consider in moments of doubt whether the seeming absence of God might be a reflection of our lives rather than a sign that there is no God. The fact that we do not see the stars at noon does not mean they are not there. Their seeming absence is a symptom of our situation rather than a sign of their demise. If our energies, affections, and efforts give little heed to the presence and purposes of God, if we consume others through unjust structures of which we are a part, then it is not surprising that we should confront a world that seems devoid of God's presence. Moments of doubt should not persuade us that we are people without faith. Doubt is a temporary dislocation, not necessarily a permanent address.

Recovery from doubt in biblical terms is a matter of the heart. God, speaking through Jeremiah, promised to cure the disloyalty of his people by a *change* of heart: "I will give them a heart to know that I am the LORD; and they shall be my people and I will be their God, for they shall return to me with their whole heart" (Jeremiah 24:7).

Again, the Lord pledged that the new covenant will be inscribed upon the heart: "But this is the covenant that I will make with the house of Israel after those days, says the LORD: I will put my law within them, and I will write it on their hearts; and I will be their God, and they shall be my people" (31:33).

The Ways of Science and the Ways of Faith

Speaking of faith and "reasons of the heart" may arouse the reluctant skeptic within each of us and make us suspicious of faith as a way of knowing God. After all, we are accustomed to thinking of faith as subjective, private opinions about which there is no objective proof. Science, on the other hand, seems to be founded on hard, indisputable facts. For example, the philosopher Bertrand Russell in his *Religion and Science* affirmed, "Whatever knowledge is attainable, must be attained by scientific methods; and what science cannot discover, mankind cannot know."[13] The glory of sci-

---

13   Bertrand Russell, *Religion and Science*, repr. and rev. ed. (New York and Oxford: Oxford University Press, 1997), 243.

ence, we usually assume, is that it is founded solely on objective facts. The sciences have of course led to many amazing breakthroughs that, used wisely, can ennoble and enhance human life. We would be mistaken, however, to view the scientific enterprise as exclusively objective efforts devoid of human interest, aspiration, and imagination. Science as it is practiced involves ample measures of imagination and the scientist's personal interests.

The familiar symbol of the world as viewed by science is the pool table. Know enough about the force and direction of any billiard ball, we think, and we can predict what will happen to other balls in its path. The world, it seems, is composed of predictable mechanical connections. We sometimes think that if we knew all the subtleties of those connections and described them objectively, the world would present us with no surprises at all.

We have already observed, however, that this mechanistic view of scientific knowing has been overturned within the scientific community itself. The world as physics views it is not the closed, minutely predictable system we sometimes picture it to be. Harvard physicist Lisa Randall reminds us that the laws of physics established in the physics of Newton break down when we consider the exceedingly minute spaces of particle physics: "Quantum mechanics tell us that electrons don't occupy fixed positions in the atoms as the classical picture would assert. Instead, probability distributions tell us how likely electrons are to be found in any particular point in space, and all we know are these probabilities. We can predict the average position of an electron as a function of time, but any particular measurement is subject to the uncertainty principle."[14]

---

14 Randall, *Knocking on Heaven's Door* (see chap. 1, n. 14).

This altered picture of the observable universe by itself changes the way we compare and contrast the ways we know in faith and the ways we know in science. We do well not to think that the physical universe is made up of billiard balls, rolling in entirely predictable ways.

Further, it is not merely the model of the physical universe that is changing. Many voices from within science itself have long challenged the view of the scientist as a dispassionate, detached student of bare facts. For example, chemist Michael Polanyi wrote decades ago that the notion of total objectivity in the sciences is a delusion.[15] Researchers are personally invested in what they investigate and which facts they consider. Evidence is selected based on what the investigator expects to find. Indeed, according to Polanyi, researchers cannot even entertain certain facts until a theory has been formed that will accommodate them. Scientists depend on a framework of understanding, a set of presuppositions about what the world is like. These presuppositions cannot be spelled out. Rather, the researcher "dwell[s] in them" in much the same way that we dwell in our own bodies.[16]

Polanyi believed that there was an inherent connection between scientific truth and beauty. The belief that a theory was true in his mind was directly related to its simplicity and elegance. The real, he thought, was also the beautiful. The intellectual beauty of mathematics was directly related in his view to its capacity to reveal a universal truth.

---

15 Michael Polanyi, *Personal Knowledge: Towards a Post-Critical Philosophy*, corr. ed. (Chicago: University of Chicago Press, 1974), 18.
16 Ibid., 60.

These considerations led Polanyi to insist that mere factuality is not science. There are only a few facts that are scientific facts. It is therefore a travesty to regard science merely as a vast neutral accumulation of data from which hypotheses can be drawn. Many great scientific discoveries, such as the Copernican system for understanding the solar system and the theory of relativity, were discovered by "pure speculation guided by criteria of internal rationality."[17] "The learner, like the discoverer, must believe before he knows."[18] This statement by Polanyi reminds us of the Anselm quote at the beginning of this chapter: "I commit myself in order that I may understand."

There is an element of trust in receiving any fact, a trust in the report itself and a reliance upon the authority of others who work in the field. While any one scientist can fully understand only a small portion of the flurry of scientific findings announced in the journals, there is a consensus that is built in the scientific community by trust in the findings of others, a "network of mutual confidence."[19]

As a scientist himself, Polanyi made none of these observations to discredit the enterprise of science itself. Rather, he was attempting to understand the way scientists actually proceed as they come to know the subject at hand. Polanyi's principal point was that scientific knowledge, as all human knowledge, includes human interest, aspiration, imagination, and assumptions about reality in attempting to understand the world. The absolute distinction

---

17   Ibid., 167.
18   Ibid., 208.
19   Ibid., 240.

between faith as subjectivity and scientific knowledge as dispassionate objectivity cannot be defended.

A similar point was made by another scientist, a physicist, Thomas Kuhn, in his enormously influential *The Structure of Scientific Revolutions*. In Kuhn's view scientific research begins with a view of what the world is fundamentally like, and this view helps to shape what questions should be asked and what observations should be considered. "Normal science . . . is predicated on the assumption that the scientific community knows what the world is like. Much of the success of the enterprise derives from the community's willingness to defend that assumption."[20] Investigators adopt models to guide their research, and their research in turn either confirms or refines them. Kuhn used the word *paradigm* to refer to comprehensive models of what the world is like. It is akin, he maintained, to a judicial decision in that it not only describes a situation or case, but it also guides how future cases are to be considered. Knowledge, in Kuhn's view, proceeds within the perspective provided by paradigms or models.

If scientists find exceptions to the prevailing paradigm, then they and the scientific community of which they are a part may either disregard those exceptions or reform the paradigm itself so that it accommodates the exceptions. Adherents or disciples are "won over" to embrace the new paradigm if it illuminates a particular situation and explains phenomena that otherwise fail to conform to prevailing theories. Schools of interpretation are built up over time, and normal research is conducted within the

---

20 Kuhn, *The Structure of Scientific Revolutions*, 5 (see chap. 5, n. 10).

parameters provided by the consensus prevailing in those scientific communities.

Kuhn's contention was that perspectives provided by the paradigm are not changed incrementally. Adherents of one paradigm cling to it even when there are observations that tend to discredit the paradigm. They persist in loyalty to the paradigm until there is another one that more fittingly interprets the data. Kuhn used the term *revolution* to refer to the process by which a scientist abandons one pattern or model in favor of another. This scientist is said to be *converted* from one paradigm to another.

Perhaps the most famous illustration of a paradigm that was held by many and then supplanted by another is the substitution of Copernican astronomy for the Ptolemaic astronomy that preceded it. The Ptolemaic astronomy, developed in the last two centuries before Christ and the first two after Christ, predicted the movements of the heavenly bodies. It assumed that the earth was the center of the universe. Through the centuries the Ptolemaic system proved to be successful in predicting the positions of the stars and the planets. Yet discrepancies did appear. In each case adjustments were made to the calculations, and it was assumed that the system could continue to be adjusted to adhere to what was actually observed. By the time of Nicolaus Copernicus (1473–1543), the Ptolemaic schema had become cumbersome and inaccurate. One predecessor of Copernicus commented that no system so cumbersome could possibly be true. After others had slowly begun to acknowledge the inadequacy of that paradigm, Copernicus wrote *De Revolutionibus* (published in 1543), in which he defended the notion that the sun was the center of the astronomical system and Earth revolved around the sun, not the reverse. New disciples were persuaded to adopt the new paradigm, obviously with great controversy, and that model became the established manner of understanding and charting the movements of the heavenly bodies. The old paradigm had failed to solve the problems of astronomy, and converts to the Copernican system believed that a competing paradigm should have a chance.[21]

Another, more recent example of a revolution or paradigm shift is the change in theories of the formation of the universe. This shift involved a significant change from the "steady state" theory of the universe to the now widely accepted theory of the "big bang" and rapid inflationary expansion of the universe. This theory and its implications will be noted in the next chapter.

We began the discussion by recognizing that in popular opinion faith is often seen merely as a subjective opinion and not based on facts. Science, on the other hand, is often viewed as strictly determined by objective facts. The view of Kuhn, Polanyi, and others on the way science works throws serious doubts on such a contrast. In the view of these scientists and many others, science is not the objective enterprise it is assumed to be. Models and paradigms in the minds of the researchers help direct and focus what we observe. They insist that data are "theory-laden," not just concrete facts registered by passive minds. The paradigms within which science works are transmitted to communities of adherents and are not themselves capable of proof. Those who work within an existing paradigm often encounter data that do not fit in with their paradigm, but this discordant note does not of itself incur distrust of the paradigm. Researchers seek out ways of interpreting

---

21 Ibid., 69–76.

the discomforting data by adjusting their observations or making incremental adjustments in the paradigm.

In the case of our knowledge of God, it is true that religious believers also interpret the world's data through paradigms that are not themselves capable of proof. The world, for example, is regarded as the creation of a provident God. Even events that seem on the surface to contradict that interpretation do not of themselves unseat the basic trust of the believer.

Against the tendency to regard science as solely objective and religion as exclusively subjective, we conclude that there are elements of both objectivity and subjectivity in each. This, of course, is not to contend that the mix of objectivity and subjectivity is equal in the fields of science and theology. For the moment we simply note that both science and religion share some parallels in the ways in which they know. At the same time, we acknowledge that in religious knowledge the role of the subjective is more prominent than in scientific knowledge.[22]

Both religion and science seek to make sense out of the world we experience. John Polkinghorne, coming from his experience both as a particle physicist and a theologian, affirms that the work of fundamental physics encounters "a world of deep and beautiful order—a universe shot through with signs of mind." He concludes, "I believe that it is indeed the Mind of that world's Creator that is perceived in this way. Science is possible because the universe is a divine creation."[23] In his view the scientific and the theological

---

22 For some of these distinctions, see Barbour, *Myths, Models and Paradigms*, 113–18. See also Ian G. Barbour, *Religion and Science: Historical and Contemporary Issues* (San Francisco: HarperCollins, 1997), 137–61.

23 Polkinghorne, *Quantum Physics and Theology*, 8 (see chap. 3, n. 21).

enterprise, while different, share a certain circularity. Both science and religion confront reality through the lenses of an interpretive point of view. That point of view (or paradigm) both illuminates and is in turn illuminated by what we observe.

Levels of Understanding

Having compared and contrasted religion and science as means of knowing, we turn now to ways of knowing that are appropriate to each. As we have seen, any level of understanding embodies some level of faith. For the scientist, that faith is the presence of order in the universe. This faith cannot be proved, but it is indispensable for the scientist's quest for truth. At that level, science can describe what actually occurs in natural phenomena, what causes are at work, and what effects are likely to follow. These observations can be tested for truth and accuracy by comparing descriptions and predictions to what actually happens.

A more complex level of understanding, however, is not merely what happens and what causes it but what it all means. The question of meaning is a new level of understanding. It deals not merely with the sequence of events in the natural world but with the purpose of there being a world at all and the question of where I as an individual fit into that world. This involves further questions, such as "Who am I?" "Do I matter in the whole scheme of things?" "Why am I here?" and "Can I make a difference?"[24] The answers to these questions are not provided by laboratory experiments or by field testing.

---

24 McGrath, *Surprised by Meaning*, 106–12 (see chap. 2, n. 5).

As an example, imagine hearing an accomplished violinist play a Beethoven sonata. One means of understanding the performance involves a description of the action of the bow on the strings, the vibrations and overtones caused by the bowing, and the acoustical principles on the amplification of sound in the instrument's sound box. Those matters can be measured and documented. But surely the performance of exquisite music is more than can be summed up in such a scientific description. At another level, the music is understood by how it moves the listener, the feelings stirred by the performance, the melodies heard in it, and the insights gained in self-understanding and purpose by means of this rendition. This second level of understanding does not violate the analysis of the physical and acoustic principles of the performance. Instead it requires a different means of understanding the reality that is there.

Similarly, we could analyze the chemical composition of a cake baked by a mother when a grown son returns home for a visit. The cake could be measured for its calories, nutritional values, weight, and so on. But at another level, the gift of a favorite dessert for a son at his homecoming has a level of significance quite separate from a scientific analysis of its ingredients and preparation. It communicates relationship and love, and missing that would be to gloss over the important meaning expressed through the cake.

Appreciating the meaning of a favorite cake or listening to a Beethoven violin sonata requires a different way of seeing and hearing than simply analyzing the chemical and acoustic properties expressed in them. It requires a way of seeing, an angle of vision, that helps the observer put this event or article in context. That way of seeing involves stories or narratives that sum up a world and define a context. It involves intentionality, decision, and involvement on the part of the observer.

These observations of meaning, in contrast to the phenomena of vibrations from a stringed instrument, are framed by stories and paradigms that put these events into context and help us appreciate the meaning to be found in them. An individual without any knowledge or appreciation of music might dismiss the violin sonata as worthless noise. An individual oblivious to loving family ties and history might spurn the cake as tasteless and unappetizing. This background and history provide a framework of understanding, a paradigm in Kuhn's language, by which the deeper meanings may be appreciated.

There is a parallel found between understanding the phenomena and causes of events and understanding their meaning. Understanding at one level is not incompatible with understanding at another level. For example, in 1859, when Charles Darwin first wrote his theory of evolution by natural selection, the controversy that ensued was not principally about the notion of evolution itself. That notion had been advanced and discussed before. What excited the greatest resistance was not the question of evolution as a process that explained the appearance of more elaborate and more specialized organisms. What stimulated resistance was the interpretation—or meaning—applied to this process. Earlier discussion of evolution carried with it the assumption that evolution was directed toward the goal of more elaborate forms of life. The process was seen to exhibit meaning and purpose. On the other hand, some came to interpret the theory of the evolution of organisms to mean that the process was devoid of meaning.[25] Neo-Darwinians such as Richard Dawkins still hold that interpretation.[26] But to provide a description of the process by which new organisms evolve and become more complex is not to answer the question of the meaning and purpose of the process by which they evolved. The question of its meaning—or lack of meaning—is not properly a scientific question.

In fact, not all contemporaries of Darwin who were Christian condemned his theory as counter to Christian faith in God's providence. In 1871 Charles Kingsley, a canon of Westminster Abbey, termed Darwin's work "a most valuable addition to natural theology." Kingsley held that creation was a process as much as it was an event. Darwin, he insisted, had clarified the mechanism by which the creation takes place. "We knew of old that God was so wise that he could make all things; but, behold, he is so much wiser than even that, that he can make all things make themselves."[27] Many Christians today interpret the theory of evolution as a credible description of the process by which God creates the world. Even Thomas Nagel, who is not a theist, questions whether the theory of evolution by itself is adequate to account for the meaning to be ascribed to the process:

> With regard to evolution, the process of natural selection cannot account for the actual history without an adequate supply of viable mutations, and I believe it remains an open

---

25 See Kuhn, *The Structure of Scientific Revolutions*, 171–72.

26 See Richard Dawkins, *The God Delusion* (Boston: Houghton Mifflin, 2006).

27 Charles Kingsley, "On the Natural Theology of the Future," in Alister McGrath, *The Passionate Intellect* (Downers Grove, IL: IVP Books, 2010), 132.

question whether this could have been provided in geological time merely as a result of chemical accident, without the operation of some other factors determining and restricting the forms of genetic variation.[28]

This discussion of competing conclusions about the meaning of evolution illustrates the difference between describing the mechanisms by which things work and the meaning of the process of which they are a part. We have described how frameworks for thinking, paradigms, serve as significant guides in exploration. We must add that such paradigms of faith are even more significant in assessing the meaning of our experience in the world. The paradigms of faith to which we refer are shaped in us by traditions and stories that provide a way for thinking about the world and its meaning.

For Christians, the Bible relates basic stories of creation, the deliverance at the Red Sea and entry into the promised land, captivity in Babylon, deliverance, the birth of Jesus Christ and his death and resurrection—all of which provide basic frameworks of understanding and meaning to our history. They become the frameworks within which we understand events. Meanings ascribed by faith to events are rooted in these fundamental stories and traditions, and they are enacted and celebrated through ritual in worship. It is in the light of these stories and rituals that we ascribe meaning and understanding to the processes and events that take place among us.

---

28 Thomas Nagel, *Mind and Cosmos: Why the Materialist Neo-Darwinian Conception of Nature Is Almost Certainly False* (New York: Oxford University Press, 2012), 8–9.

Conclusion

In this chapter we have discussed the nature of our knowledge of God given through faith and how this knowledge compares and contrasts with the findings of science. We turn in the next chapter to consider how the affirmations of faith are confirmed by the light they shed in making sense out of the universe as we experience it.

REFLECTION QUESTIONS

1. In your view is the experience of doubt a failing on your part or an occasion for deeper reflection, study, and examination? How do you respond to doubt?

2. Do you agree with the astronomer who said that you cannot believe what you think is untrue? Or is belief for you a matter that is to be accepted, even if one is not assured that it is true?

3. What does it mean to say that faith must be lived before it is understood? Can you think of any elements of your faith that originated in an experience or experiences rather than in pure thought?

4. Do you agree that there are things we cannot imagine that are nonetheless true? Can you think of examples out of your experience? How does this apply or fail to apply to our belief about God?

5. How would you say that religious conversion is comparable to paradigm changes in science? Have you observed such changes in your own attitudes and beliefs? Have you seen

them in others? Can you point to what prompted these changes?

6. Have you had experiences in which you trusted a friend or loved one even when, at least temporarily, you did not understand something he or she said or did? Is this an example of believing in order to understand? How does this apply to our trust in God?

Faith Seeking Explanation

*Ever since the creation of the world his eternal power and divine nature,
invisible though they are, have been understood and seen through the
things he has made.*

—Romans 1:20

*If I light an electric torch at night out of doors,
I don't judge its power by looking at the bulb,
but by seeing how many objects it lights up. . . .
The value of a religious . . .
way of life is appreciated by the amount of illumination
thrown upon the things of this world.*

—Simone Weil, *First and Last Notebooks*

We understood faith in the previous chapter as a necessary ingredient in understanding, and we have compared and contrasted faith and science as ways of knowing. We hold that understanding the world around us requires us to rely on convictions that we cannot prove. Earlier we noted Lesslie Newbigin's contention that "we do not come to know anything except by believing something."[1] Newbigin added, "The great scientific theories take as their starting point some belief about what is ultimate and fundamental in their area of study. In other words, they start from a belief about what religious people call 'god.'"[2]

Both religion and science, as we have seen, search as truth-seeking communities for explanations of the world employing paradigms or models of the way the world operates. In the case of scientific explorations, those paradigms guide the researcher in further discovery. Scientific revolutions occur when the realities observed no longer fit meaningfully into the prevailing models. Similarly, religious faith embodies certain models for understandings of the world, and truth-seeking communities of faith explore the manner in which that faith sheds light on life and history. "We are not . . . looking," John Polkinghorne reminds us, "to the physical world for hints of God's existence but to God's existence as an aid for understanding why things have developed in the physical world in the manner that they have."[3]

The paradigm used by people of faith has been shaped and refined by conversations and debates over the generations. For example, the Jewish and Christian communities over time have viewed the physical world as a creation of God. Creation accounts have affirmed that the physical world originates with and is dependent upon the providence and sustenance of God. The person of

---

1   Newbigin, *Truth and Authority in Modernity*, 3 (see chap. 4, n. 1).

2   Ibid., 10.

3   John Polkinghorne, *Belief in God in an Age of Science* (New Haven, CT: Yale University Press, 1998), 13.

faith participates in the search for explanation with a conviction about what is ultimate and with confidence that this faith will lead to greater understanding and explanation.

The search of faith for explanation, then, involves the conviction that the narrative of faith in which we stand bears the truth and makes sense within itself. We also stand in the expectation, like those who employ other paradigms and narratives about the world, that the Word of faith will lead us to further understanding about the world. Faith seeks explanation.

Seeking the Best Explanation

There is a venerable tradition that seeks to begin with universal statements that cannot be denied. This is often called *foundationalism*. Using a metaphor from building, it suggests that we base our search for the truth of God's existence on truths with which everyone would have to agree. Further arguments are built on that foundation. For example, we could argue that everything that exists came into being from the action of some prior cause. From that we could argue that to understand the world, we must acknowledge a First Cause, or God. On that foundation we could build a fuller concept of who this God, this First Cause, actually is. This approach to proving the existence of God has a long lineage and has helped define the logic of faith. It assumes that our explanation of God begins "from the ground up" and rests on conclusions with which any reasonable person would have to agree. In fact, it may be a better *expression* of belief than proof of the existence of God. However effective this argument is in voicing the logic of belief, it seldom reflects the way we actually *come* to belief or persuade others to do so.[4]

In our natural reasoning, and in science, we often use another way of seeking explanation. In this we take three steps: (1) We observe a happening that calls for explanation. (2) We reason that if a certain theory were true, this happening would be readily understandable. (3) We conclude that this provides reason to believe that the theory is true.[5] This general approach may be used as well among people of faith. On examination there are striking features of the world that call for explanation. We may show that if the world is the creation of God, those features will be readily understandable. This in turn gives us further reason to conclude that faith in God is justified and true.

To be sure, reasoning does not reach incontrovertible "proof" of the truth of what we believe. However, it does represent the most adequate explanation for what would otherwise be difficult to explain. The truth of the explanation that is offered is not determined by unshakable foundations that no one could challenge. Rather, the affirmation that is defended in this matter is confirmed by the way it fits meaningfully with other experience of the world. If it fits with or is coherent with surrounding experience, that is yet

---

4   An important exception is the philosopher Antony Flew, a famous and well-published exponent of atheism, who at the end of his life published *There Is a God* (New York: HarperCollins, 2007). In this publication he changed his long-held conviction on atheism and concluded, as the title implies, that God is real. He stated at the end of the book that the cosmological argument is a "promising explanation, probably the finally right one" (p. 145).

5   This illustration by Charles Peirce is cited in Alister E. McGrath, *A Fine-Tuned Universe* (Louisville: Westminster John Knox Press, 2009), 45. Peirce (1839–1914) referred to this method as "abduction." See pp. 45–55.

further reason to believe it to be true. The metaphor used for this line of reason contrasts with "foundation" and instead is called the *web*. The web connects with and fits into a surrounding body of experience and conviction.[6]

The explanation provided by this argument is not absolute proof. But venturing in trust beyond what can be proved is an intrinsic quality of faith itself. Inclusive accounts of the world, its origins and purposes, we can argue, are not capable of proof. We listen again to Alfred Lord Tennyson (1809–92) from his *Ancient Sage*:

> Thou canst not prove thou art immortal, no,
> Nor yet that thou art mortal—nay my son,
> Thou canst not prove that I, who speak with thee,
> Am not thyself in converse with thyself,
> *For nothing worthy proving can be proven,*
> Nor yet disproven: wherefore thou be wise,
> Cleave ever to the sunnier side of doubt.
> (Emphasis added)

People who believe in God walk in trust and faith rather than absolute proof. What we do seek is the confirmation through reasoning that belief in God provides the best explanation for why the world is as it is and how we may live creatively within it. The light I gain from what I believe does not prove the truth of the belief. But

---

6   For discussions of the web metaphor, see Nancey Murphy, "Bridging Theology and Science in a Postmodern Age," in *Bridging Science and Religion,* ed. Ted Peters and Gaymon Bennett (Minneapolis: Fortress Press, 2003), 45–46. See also Stanley J. Grenz and John R. Franke, *Beyond Foundationalism* (Louisville: John Knox Press, 2001), 38ff.

it does help to give grounds for believing that what we hold to be true is reliable and trustworthy for the living of a life. It is an "inference to the best explanation."[7]

In scientific research an investigator will often remain loyal to informing paradigms or models even when there are anomalies and questions that are still to be answered by further experience. Charles Darwin acknowledged that there were questions about natural selection and the transmission of acquired characteristics that he had not yet explained. Yet he insisted that the greater number of the unresolved issues were "only apparent, and that those that are real are not, I think, fatal to my theory."[8] To be sure, there are certain findings of science that are subject to proof. But the big questions about the origin and destiny of the universe do not lend themselves to definitive proof. Theorists in this field may be confident that what is believed today may require to be changed in the future. Standard science textbooks remind students that "science rests on faith."[9] This is not to say that broad convictions about God and the world are comparable in all regards to scientific theories. What they do share, however, is the pursuit of understanding that leads to the most adequate explanation.

One further word must be said about the way we seek the best explanation. We are looking for an explanation that places God both in and above the world and not merely as one entity within

---

7   A phrase used by Peter Lipton as the title of his 2004 publication and cited in McGrath, *A Fine-Tuned Universe,* 53.

8   Charles Darwin, *On the Origin of Species by Means of Natural Selection, or The Preservation of Favoured Races in the Struggle for Life,* 3rd ed., with additions and corrections (London: John Murray, 1861), 189.

9   Hugh G. Gauch Jr., *Scientific Method in Practice* (New York: Cambridge University Press, 2002), 151–52. See also pp. 1–110.

the world. The God of the biblical narrative transcends the world, but God is also involved in the world as Creator and Sustainer. Some suggest that we should think of the world as God's body. God transcends the world as the mind transcends the body. Yet God is related to and involved in the world as the mind is involved in the body. The analogy has significant limits, but it does provide the suggestion of God who is related to but not confined by the world.

In searching for explanation, we should not presume that any explanations will eliminate all mystery and uncertainty. At times in the history of the church, believing people have attempted to use the concept of God to answer questions that the science of the day could not answer. This "God of the gaps," as it is called, is a very tenuous enterprise. First, it is unsatisfactory because as scientific knowledge increases, there is less need for a God who explains only what we do not understand by other means. Perhaps more serious, however, is the misunderstanding of God that it represents. God is not an entity that may or may not be added to the world around us. God is instead the Creator, the origin, the ground of the world and all that is within it.[10] It is not as if we could observe the world as it is and then decide whether God is an optional element in that world. In biblical perspective, God moves in and through all the world, not in absolute detachment from the world or as one article or cause among many.

We err when we think that a description of the natural processes by which the world comes to be precludes the need for God. To people of faith the natural processes may well be the means by which God guides and sustains creation. Someone observing a

---

10 McGrath, *The Passionate Intellect*, 110 (see chap. 7, n. 27).

sprinkler in which children are playing on a hot day may detail the water pressure, the system that delivers the water, the pumps, the garden hose, and other material causes. Those all are pertinent to the scene observed. But this description does not preclude the fact that all these forces and facts are put into action by the love of a parent who wants his or her children to enjoy cooling off and playing in the water on a hot day. To describe the natural processes of the world does not preclude the possibility that they are expressions of a provident and loving Creator. English scientist Charles Coulson expressed it in these terms: "Either God is in the whole of Nature, with no gaps, or He's not there at all."[11]

In the following sections of this chapter, we will look at some of the noteworthy features of the universe and attempt to show how they may be understood in the context of Christian belief. If convictions of faith provide the most sensible explanation for these surprising facts—if in the context of faith those observations are not surprising but are understandable—then the explanation provided will furnish additional grounds for believing that the convictions of faith are firmly grounded in the way things are. We turn to several notable observations of the world and the questions that arise from them.

First Cause: Why Is There Anything?

We have mentioned that one attempted proof of God springs from the universe, and anything else that exists must have had a

---

11 C. A. Coulson, *Science and Christian Belief* (Chapel Hill, NC: University of North Carolina Press, 1955), 22.

cause and a beginning. That cause, the argument goes, must be other than the universe, and that cause is God. This line of reasoning argument has a history that may be traced to Thomas Aquinas in the thirteenth century.

We acknowledged that while this argument is an explanation of faith in God, it fails to convince or persuade everyone. Some, for example, insist that there is no reason that everything must have a cause. Something may just exist, and this need not be termed God. Perhaps the universe just exists as an impersonal entity.[12] In fact, during the first decades of the twentieth century, the dominant scientific viewpoint held that the universe had always existed and was eternal. In that period notions of a "creation" were regarded by many as purely mythological and unscientific. Atheist thinker Bertrand Russell thought that the idea of the steady state universe that had always existed was sufficient reason to put to rest the notion of God.[13] The prevalent view was that the universe is just there and that no explanation of its origin was needed.

In the 1920s, however, Edwin Hubble (1889–1953) demonstrated that the universe was not observed to be a steady state and that it was in fact expanding at a rapid and accelerating rate of speed. If the universe had been expanding for billions of years, this led to the conclusion that it began in a very compact and dense state. This meant that the universe in fact had a beginning.

Though there was resistance to the idea that the universe had a beginning, the consensus began to change in the 1960s when researchers discovered with their microwave antennae a

---

12   John Hick, *Between Faith and Doubt: Dialogues on Religion and Reason* (New York: Macmillan, 2010), 15.
13   McGrath, *Why God Won't Go Away*, 127.

background hissing noise throughout the cosmos. Extensive investigations led to the conclusion that this background noise was the "afterglow" of an initial cosmic explosion about which there had been speculation in earlier years. This initial event came to be known, at first as a term of derision by doubters, as the "big bang."[14] The idea of a fiery beginning to an expanding universe was resisted extensively by many scientists of the day. Albert Einstein was one of those who resisted some of the results of his own investigations and clung for a time to the notion that the universe was eternal and unchanging.[15] Astrophysicist Fred Hoyle initially opposed the big bang theory on the grounds that it sounded "religious."[16]

The prevailing view of the expansion of the universe from the size of an atom is known as the *inflationary cosmology*. In the exceptional circumstances of the big bang, the force of gravity acted as a repulsive force in time sequences that one researcher has said would make a nanosecond (one billionth of a second) "seem an eternity."[17] In that event, thought to have taken place 13.7 billion years ago, the universe inflated at unimaginable speeds, and continues these billions of years later to accelerate its expansion at speeds varying (depending upon their distance from the earth) between 5.5 million miles per hour and 16.5 million miles per hour.[18]

The scientific community resisted the notion that the universe was expanding, even though, as astrophysicist Robert Jastrow reminds us, five independent lines of evidence all indicate that the

---

14 McGrath, *A Fine-Tuned Universe*, 113–14.
15 Greene, *The Fabric of the Cosmos*, 274 (see chap. 2, n. 4).
16 McGrath, *Why God Won't Go Away*, 127.
17 Greene, *The Fabric of the Cosmos*, 273.
18 Ibid., 229.

universe in fact had a beginning.[19] He noted that science has faith in the order and harmony of the universe. In this faith every event must have a previous cause. Science can prove that the universe exploded at a certain moment, but there is no scientific answer for the question, who or what put matter and energy in the universe? "The scientist's pursuit of the past," wrote Jastrow, "ends in the moment of creation." There may be an explanation for the explosive origin of our universe, but it is not attainable by science. Such a notion, concluded Jastrow, is strange and "unexpected by all but the theologians." They have always believed that in the beginning God created the heaven and earth.[20]

We should note that the growing consensus gave new significance to the long-held argument that God was the First Cause of the universe. Some of those who held to the steady state theory thought it unnecessary to think of a First Cause for the universe. It was just there. The typical answer to viewing God as the First Cause was to ask, "What caused God?" The first cause argument for God had been that whatever exists has a cause. William Lane Craig and others have rephrased the argument to say "whatever begins to exist has a cause." It is now generally agreed, as we have seen, that the world did in fact *begin* in an instant to exist. The world, therefore—unlike God, who is eternal—did have a beginning and thus must have a cause.[21]

19　These five lines of evidence are: "the motions of the galaxies, the discovery of the primordial fireball, the laws of thermodynamics, the abundance of helium in the Universe and the life story of the stars." Robert Jastrow, *God and the Astronomers*, 2nd ed. (New York: W. W. Norton, 1992), 106.

20　Ibid., 106.

21　William Lane Craig, *Reasonable Faith*, 3rd ed. (Wheaton, IL: Crossway, 2003), 111ff.

The point in referring to the rather dramatic reversal in science to view the world as having a beginning is not to claim the book of Genesis as a scientific textbook. It is not. The book of Genesis does not pretend to describe the mechanisms through which God created the world. Affirmations of the Bible are expressed in poetic form, not in the language of astrophysics. In fact, Genesis contains two accounts of the creation. The first (1:1–2:4), considered to have been written in Babylon in the sixth century BCE, represents the world as issuing forth from God's initiating action. It counters the Babylonian myths of creation and stresses instead the transcendence of God, who creates by the divine word, the dignity of humans as trustees of the rest of creation, and the orderliness of the creation in place of chaos. An older account of the creation (2:4-25) assumed its present form in about 900 BCE. It affirms the order of the creation and stresses that man and woman were created in the image of God and given responsibility for caring for the creation. In the second century BCE there was an added emphasis on the affirmation that God created the universe out of nothing (*ex nihilo*).[22] Clement of Alexandria (c. 150–215) later gave fuller expression to the idea of creation *ex nihilo*, saying that the notion of an eternal cosmos was idolatrous. The idea of an eternal cosmos, he held, made nature a second coeternal God. In its place, he argued for the view that the universe emerged from the "sheer volition of God."[23]

The point of describing this shift to holding that the universe had a beginning is not cited to "prove" the Genesis account(s) of

---

22 Hans Küng, *The Beginning of All Things: Science and Religion.* trans. John Bowden (Grand Rapids, MI: Wm. B. Eerdmans, 2007), 115–16.
23 Armstrong, *The Case for God,* 104 (see chap. 4, n. 2).

the creation. Once again, the stories of the creation are poetic testimonies of faith and not scientific reports. Rather, our interest is to show that our faith in God throws light on the mystery of creation, upon what preceded the "big bang." To the person of faith, it is quite comprehensible that God created the world out of divine freedom and that the order and patterns found in the creation reflect the divine intention. The harmony or consonance between the biblical account and the best scientific explanations, while not proof of the biblical account, does illustrate how that account provides a sensible way to understand why and by whom the earth came to be.

Creation: Is Creation Both an Event and a Process?

Insights from Christian faith and from contemporary science are causing us also to rethink our views about the creation. Customarily we think of a singular event in which the world came into being with plants, animals, and humans inhabiting the world pretty much as we see them today. In the eighteenth century people tended to think of the world as an artifact, and God was viewed as the designer of God's handiwork. They often spoke of God as the watchmaker and the intricacy of the creation as the watchmaker's handiwork. The complexity of the design represented the skill and intelligence of the watchmaker who made it. William Paley's *Natural Theology* (1802) outlined the manner in which the world as it was created showed the hand of its creator.

One result of Charles Darwin's *Origin of Species* (1859) was to challenge the notion of the universe as a fixed work and to replace it with a notion of the universe as a process of flux and change. The species appeared as they are, according to Darwin's theory, not as a result of a fixed creation but as the product of millions of years of adaptation and change. Some interpreted this new thought to mean that the living organisms of their world represented not the products of the hand of God but rather the result of random change, natural selection, and survival of the fittest.

It was the implication that the process of evolution was devoid of direction and purpose that concerned many of Darwin's contemporaries. Yet there were those even in the early discussions of evolution who understood this theory not as a denial of God's action but as a description of the manner in which God creates. We have seen how theologian Charles Kingsley in 1871 interpreted evolution as the means God utilizes to "make all things make themselves."[24] In place of a static view of creation, Kingsley held that God's creative activity was to be seen in God's continuing presence and providence in the evolving natural order.

The notion of God's creation as a continuing process rather than a singular event fits coherently with understandings of God in the Bible. The God portrayed in the biblical records cannot be confined simply to a role like that of a watchmaker who creates a fixed product and remains somewhat detached from the natural order. In contrast, the prologue to John's Gospel portrays God's Word as the principle and vehicle of creation. "All things came into being through him. . . . What has come into being in him was life, and the life was the light of all people" (1:3-4). The writer of Psalm

---

24 Charles Kingsley, "The Natural Theology of the Future," in McGrath, *A Fine-Tuned Universe*, 168.

104 pictured God as the Creator who is intimately involved in the life of God's creation:

> These all look to you
> > to give them their food in due season;
> when you give to them, they gather it up;
> > when you open your hand they are filled with good things.
> When you hide your face, they are dismayed;
> > when you take away their breath, they die
> > and return to their dust.
> When you send forth your spirit, they are created;
> > and you renew the face of the ground. (vv. 27-30)

For the believer the notion of God as the continuing Creator is supported by trends within science itself. Modern science had been dominated in the past by an approach that reduced every object to its constituent parts and sought from those parts to reconstruct it. Yet the direction of more recent nuclear physics and biology is to understand entities as whole systems and to see them in relationship with their environment and surroundings. They understand and interpret entities in their relationships rather than by reducing them into irreducible and static parts.[25]

A key issue that confronts any student of the universe is whether the changes that take place do so with any direction or purpose. Is the evolving world simply the product of random and purposeless activity, or is there intentionality and purpose to be found in apparently random activities? The notion of purpose, of

---

25 Jürgen Moltmann, *God in Creation,* trans. Margaret Kohl (San Francisco: Harper & Row, 1985), 2–3.

course, is dismissed immediately by the so-called New Atheists. Richard Dawkins, for example, labels any effort to discern purpose as "childish."[26]

The only purpose of evolution, according to Dawkins, is the propagation of one's genes into the next generation. It is important to recognize that this denial of any intentionality in the universe is not a verdict of science itself but rather represents a belief reached on unscientific grounds. It is hardly surprising that one who has a prior commitment to atheism would fail to find purpose in creation. Other scientists who do not share this atheistic belief may interpret the universe and changes within it as the work of a divine Creator who guides the world in a process of evolving and progressing toward fulfillment of the divine intentions for the world. There is nothing incompatible, in this view, between apparent random activity and the purposes of God in creation.

While some deny the evidence of any purpose in the continuing process of an evolving world, there are significant challenges to this point of view that are taking place in the science of evolution itself. These challenges point to evidences of direction in the paths of evolution. The process of evolution, these voices insist, does not reflect sheer random change. It appears that chemical forces themselves created a "channel," directing evolution from single-celled organisms into plants and animals.[27]

Is it plausible, some challengers ask, that the action of pure chance and the laws of chemistry could produce self-reproducing complex life forms on the earth? Further, they ask, what is the

---

26 Dawkins, *The God Delusion*, 181 (see chap. 7, n. 26).
27 McGrath, *A Fine-Tuned Universe*, 156.

source of variations or genetic mutations that are necessary to produce the organisms that are to be found on the earth? One such critic, Thomas Nagel, gives away his answer to these questions through the subtitle of his book: *Mind and Cosmos: Why the Materialist Neo-Darwinian Conception of Nature Is Almost Certainly False.*[28]

We will return later in the discussion to the evidence of what we will now just call a bias toward life in the unfolding story of the process of creation. At this point, it is important to recognize that the description of creation as a process as well as an event in no way restricts our ability to view it as a sign of God's creative work. The identification of change taking place through the generation of mutations and adaptation through natural selection does not require us to interpret this as sheer chance. It is more plausible to regard it simply as the process through which God continues to create the world.

Chemist and theologian Alister McGrath, for example, points out that it is quite plausible to hold that God created water. Furthermore, this affirmation is compatible with the scientific process by which water, a simple compound of hydrogen and oxygen, was created. Hydrogen could not form until the embryonic universe had cooled from the initial explosion. Oxygen could not be formed until gases, billions of years later, had coalesced and formed stars, and those stars had developed the critical mass to synthesize or fuse the heavier elements, such as oxygen. The combination of hydrogen and oxygen originally was found solely in the gaseous state and only much later condensed into its liquid form. When

---

28 Nagel, *Mind and Cosmos*, 6 (see chap. 7, n. 28).

we speak of God creating water, therefore, we are not speaking of a singular event when this basic ingredient of life appeared, but of processes extending over billions of years. Water is termed a late arrival in the creation, but processes and laws established in the universe assured that it would eventually make its appearance in the created order. To the eyes of faith, God is active in setting forth the conditions and guiding the process by which water came to be.[29]

The ability to view creation as both an event and a process helps the person of faith to explain the whole unfolding movement from a dense and unimaginably hot state to the creation we see today. The hand of God is seen not only in the initiation of the process but in the laws and constraints that have been found to have guided the process. The presence of stars to fuse carbon, the generation of mutations, and the ability to encode genetic information and pass it on to future generations are only some of the variables that help account for life.

For much of the modern period, it was unfashionable to refer to any purpose in the creation but to regard it only as the development of a pointless process of chance. Now science itself is beginning to talk about signs of purpose and intent. Far from being a scattershot process, evolution appears to be "converging" upon a limited number of possible goals. Paleobiologist Simon Conway Morris holds that the process of evolving is focused on evolutionary outcomes that act as "attractors" in apparent chaos. The evolution of photosynthesis, for example, has been shown to have evolved independently at least thirty-one times. The formation of

---

29 McGrath, *A Fine-Tuned Universe,* 212.

eyes in animals has developed independently and in various ways in multiple contexts. Evolution shows, Morris holds, that it is a process that focuses on a limited number of end points and converges upon a relatively small set of solutions to problems confronted in the environment.[30]

At this point our intention is not to prove the existence of God from the appearance of direction in the created order. It is rather to suggest that believing in God gives us a way of understanding and explaining the signs of convergence and intent evident in the process of evolution. Believing in God also helps us understand creation not only as a fiery beginning 13.7 billion years ago but as an ongoing process in which God continues to act and guide the process. God goes beyond and transcends the creation, but God is also found guiding and luring the creation forward. The complexity, beauty, and order of the universe are qualities that do not come as a surprise to the person who believes in God. The beginning of all things and their continuing development are explicable as the handiwork of a loving and creative God.

Human Life: Did the Universe Know We Were Coming?

Reference to the direction in the course of evolution raises the question of purpose and design at the very beginning of the universe. Scientists have discovered and pointed out for us a remarkable set of fine tolerances present in the first microsecond of the creation that made life possible. This constellation of remarkably

---

30 Simon Conway Morris, *Life's Solution: Inevitable Humans in a Lonely Universe* (Cambridge: Cambridge University Press, 2003), in McGrath, *A Fine-Tuned Universe*, 192–93.

close tolerances has been referred to since 1974 as the *anthropic principle*. This term, formed from the Greek word for human, has come to refer to the finely tuned circumstances in the universe that made human life possible over billions of years, first in the primitive forms of life and eventually in the appearance of human beings. The term reflects wonder and surprise that a host of intricate variations could appear to be aligned so masterfully to make human life possible. The theoretical physicist Freeman Dyson famously remarked, "The more I examine the universe and the details of its architecture, the more evidence I find that the universe in some sense must have known that we were coming."[31]

In chapter 3 we cited one illustration of the extraordinarily fine tolerances necessary for creating a universe hospitable for human life. As a further illustration, we could note the finely tuned rate of inflation that made it possible for the universe to expand. Stephen Hawking has written that if the expansion rate following the big bang were smaller even by one part in a hundred thousand million million, the universe would have collapsed upon itself and never achieved its current size. Conversely, if the expansion rate had been greater by one part in a million, the universe would have expanded so rapidly that stars and galaxies could not have formed. Harvard astronomer Owen Gingerich estimates that the initial rate of expansion had to be accurate to about one part in ten followed by fifty-nine zeros in order to allow the universe to expand as it has.[32] Had the stars and the galaxies not formed, the universe

---

31 Freeman Dyson, *Disturbing the Universe*, Sloan Foundation Science Series ed. (New York: Harper & Row, 1981), 250.

32 Owen Gingerich, *God's Universe* (Cambridge, MA: Harvard University Press, 2006), 49.

would never have formed carbon, the basic building block of life, or other heavy elements that are fused in the nuclear furnace of the stars.

Again, we have noted that if the strong nuclear force (one of the fundamental forces in the universe, along with the weak nuclear force, electromagnetic force, and gravity) were weaker in the slightest degree, we would have only hydrogen in the universe. If the strong nuclear force were minimally stronger, all the hydrogen would have been converted to helium. In either situation, there would have been no stable stars and compounds such as water.[33]

John Polkinghorne tells of his fellow physicist Fred Hoyle, who studied the intricate processes necessary to produce carbon. He learned the delicate process of combining helium and fusing it with beryllium and established that if the laws of physics had been changed in the slightest degree, there could have been no carbon. Hoyle, according to Polkinghorne, has a "lifetime inclination to atheism." Yet he concluded that such remarkable fine-tuning could not be an accident. Hoyle did not care to use the word "God," but he concluded that there must be "cosmic intelligence behind it all."[34]

The scientific literature in the field enumerates six knife-edge balances in the physical universe, any alteration of which would have made human life impossible.[35] However, perhaps these illustrations may suggest the point to be made. The universe at its very beginning was constituted with laws and principles that were intricately balanced in a bias toward life. The questions it raises are:

---

33 Barbour, *Religion and Science*, 204–5 (see chap. 7, n. 22).
34 Polkinghorne, *Quarks*, 41 (see chap. 2, n. 14).
35 Summarized in McGrath, *A Fine-Tuned Universe*, 119.

How is it that basic laws and forces in the universe are balanced in such a delicate manner that makes life possible? Is chance an adequate explanation?

One has asked what we would think if we walked into a room and saw a Scrabble game that apparently had been scattered aimlessly on the floor. What would be our response if on further inspection we saw amid the scattered tiles a perfectly aligned row of tile that spelled out a line from Shakespeare's *Hamlet*? Would this suggest some intervention beyond sheer chance at work?

Within the framework of faith, the bias toward life built into the basic structure of the universe certainly suggests a formative hand at work. While not a proof of divine intention, that possibility certainly springs to mind. Within the context of faith, it is perfectly comprehensible that the universe as it is shows signs of intentionality and providential guidance in the flow of creation. If faith in God helps illuminate the processes we actually see at work, the congruence of what we believe and what we observe gives further confidence that faith in God is well founded.

Of course, this is not the only possible response to the apparent direction of the universe in favor of life. We observed earlier in the discussion that some theorists with a prior commitment against theistic belief propose the rather extravagant notion that there is not one universe but an unimaginable number of universes. They suggest, as we have seen, that it "just happens" that the one in which we live by chance presents just the right combination of variables to make life possible. Those hypothetical universes, of course, have not and never could be observed. Nevertheless, they theorize that with billions of hypothetical universes, pure chance could result in just the right balance exhibited in this, the one universe that we know.

Some exponents of this view have pointed out that it has the advantage of avoiding any claims for divine guidance in the evolution of life. We observed earlier, for example, that Massachusetts Institute of Technology physicist Alan Lightman dismisses any claim of divine leading in the course of evolution on the grounds that this theory "does not appeal to most scientists." He holds that the multiuniverse theory, on the other hand, offers a way to explain the apparent fine-tuning of the universe without "the presence of a Designer." He sides with his fellow scientist Steven Weinberg, who argues that through the multiuniverse theory we can understand why we live in a universe favorable to life without relying on the benevolence of a creator.[36] For some, therefore, it appears that the multiuniverse theory is in part a speculative theory to avoid the threat of theism. Whatever the motivation for the multiuniverse claim, however, it does strain credulity to imagine billions of unseen universes proposed as an explanation for the bias toward life to be observed in our own. In the eyes of faith, it is far more plausible to interpret the exquisite balance in favor of life as a sign of intentionality and purpose in a divine Creator and Sustainer of the universe.

Emergence: Did Mind Come from Matter?

A quick look at the world around us readily shows us that it is made of many different levels of things. We mingle with rocks and soil.

---

36 Alan Lightman, "The Accidental Universe," 37–38 (see chap. 1, n. 15)

We interact with living plants that take in nourishment and grow. We relate to other people, and we entertain thoughts, emotions, hopes, and dreams. We learn that our bodies are formed with molecules of carbon that were fused in the furnaces of the stars. We learn that our brains, with their 85 billion neurons, are easily the most complicated instrument in creation. Neurologists tell us that thoughts, feelings, and emotions are triggered by the firing of these neurons in the brain. Yet there is a keen difference between my consciousness of feeling for a loved one, for example, and clinical descriptions of neural firing in the lobes of the brain. Is the mind, and the thoughts entertained by it, nothing more than the electrical activity in the brain?

This introduces the question of strata or distinct levels within the natural order. The material world is made up of strata or levels, each level exhibiting qualities that were not present in the preceding level. When chemicals interact with one another, a product emerges that could not have been predicted before their interaction. For example, salt is made up by combining sodium and chloride. Sodium is a silvery metal; chloride is a greenish-yellow gas. Nothing in the two chemicals could have helped us predict the properties that emerged from their interaction.[37] Salt exists as a potential outcome for sodium and chloride, but that potential could not have been predicted from the elements themselves.

The principle by which complex structures organize into new structures that previously did not exist is called *emergence*. Each level has links to its antecedents, yet it exhibits characteristics that distinguish it from the level or stratum from which they developed.

---

37 McGrath, *A Fine-Tuned Universe*, 206.

Our world is filled with emergent creations. "Emergence," says Michael Gazzaniga, is the process in which "micro-level complex systems that are far from equilibrium . . . self-organize . . . into new structures, with new properties that previously did not exist, to form a new level of organization on the macro level."[38]

The natural world presents us with elements that are of several strata or levels. They form a hierarchy of complexity and organization that according to one author includes: inorganic being, matter; organic being, with organisms including metabolism and reproduction; mental beings with consciousness; and spiritual beings with thought, knowledge, and personality.[39] Some tend to explain each level in terms of its links to the antecedent level to explain causes from the "bottom up." For example, some interpret morality and ethical judgments fundamentally as the functioning of an inborn drive to reproduce and preserve one's genes. Supposedly altruistic behavior is said by them to be simply an attempt to strengthen our tribe or family group. Those endorsing this interpretation explain the mind only as the activity of the electrical apparatus of the brain. Complex and supposedly higher functioning is interpreted without remainder as an expression of its antecedents.

But this is not the only way emergence can be interpreted. Upper levels may exhibit distinctive qualities over their antecedents and thus be said to exercise supervenience over them. For example, imagine a painting like Leonardo da Vinci's *Mona Lisa*. One level of the painting is a description of the chemicals, oils, dyes, and brushstrokes that compose it. But a description of those

---

38 Gazzaniga, *Who's in Charge?*, 124 (see chap. 2, n. 10).
39 Nicolai Hartman, in ibid., 213.

ingredients would in no way convey the beauty of the painting itself. The emergent develops properties not found in its antecedents.

Beyond this supervenience of meaning, however, is a certain *top-down* connection of the higher and lower levels of complexity. In biofeedback and the placebo phenomenon, for example, the mind exercises downward causation and influence on the body. The higher level exercises causation on the lower. At a much different level, the function of a cell determines the behavior of the macromolecules of which it is constructed. In each case the emergent exhibits qualities and functions not to be found in its antecedent level.[40]

All of this raises serious questions about a purely materialistic or naturalistic interpretation of our universe. We return to questions asked before. How does it happen, we are entitled to ask, that sheer matter gives birth to living things and to organisms that are conscious, thinking, willing, and feeling? How is it possible for materials fused in the stars to be aware and think about where they fit into the whole cosmic order? If these characteristics and capacities emerged from the natural order, wasn't the potential for such an emergence inherent in the natural order that gave them birth?[41]

Running through all these questions is the issue of reductionism. Some hold, as we have seen, that we can understand each level by breaking it down to a lower level. The process of thinking, for example, is to be understood solely as chemical and electrical

---

40 James W. Jones, *Can Science Explain Religion? The Cognitive Science Debate* (New York: Oxford University Press, 2016), 156–58.

41 Some of these questions are raised in Nagel, *Mind and Cosmos*, 31–32 (see chap. 7, n. 28).

activity of the organism. Philosopher Thomas Nagel forcefully argues against this notion. The world creates individuals who think, he insists. Moral and logical forms of reasoning are valid and are not just the expression of material forces operating within us. Mind and reasons are basic and not merely derivatives.[42] An adequate theory of human experience, he holds, would have to include an explanation of how these mental elements are inherent in life and not the expression of purely physical forces. We can't just argue, according to Nagel, that evolution produced consciousness. We must explain *how* evolution produced consciousness. We need an explanation of how the potentiality for consciousness was present from the beginning.[43] Clearly there had to be a potentiality for mental activity and consciousness that explains the experience of thinking and shows how it is not just a product of random causes.

We are looking at this question in the present discussion to illustrate observations that call for an explanation. It is interesting that Nagel, who argues so convincingly for an explanation for consciousness and thought that goes beyond mere random chance, rules out any explanation that involves divine creation. He grants that the theologically minded can find an explanation through a divine intelligence who has created the potential for mind in the divine guidance of the process of evolution. He even agrees that there is ample reason for this conclusion. But he leaves the question up in the air. He prefers an answer that does not involve God, he says, because it is "congruent with my atheism."[44] His prior world-view and existing paradigm precludes his following the evidence of

---

42 Ibid., 30–32.
43 Ibid., 65.
44 Ibid., 95.

divine intelligence that works in and through the creation to guide the creation into levels of higher complexity and meaning.

In an earlier writing Nagel made this point with startling and striking candor. He admitted that prior commitments and mind-sets keep him from following the evidence to belief in God. He confessed in that earlier writing to a "fear of religion." He wants, he says, for atheism to be true: "It isn't just that I don't believe in God and, naturally, hope that I'm right in my belief. It's that I hope there is no God! I don't want the universe to be like that. . . . I am curious whether there is anyone who is genuinely indifferent as to whether there is a God—anyone who, whatever his actual belief about the matter, doesn't particularly *want* either one of the answers to be correct."[45]

We sometimes hear opponents of faith in God dismiss belief as wish fulfillment. Here we hear the remarkable testimony of one whose disbelief in God is obviously and self-confessedly a product of his wishes on the matter.

Perhaps Nagel is correct in holding that when it comes to belief or nonbelief in God, we all have our wishes in the matter. No doubt we who believe would *like* to believe that the world and all who live herein are creatures of a gracious and providential God whose will is for the good of all the creation. Yet at this point it is not our preferences on the matter that are in question. When it comes to faith seeking explanation, we are seeking to determine whether the trust we have invested in the God who for us is known in Jesus Christ is a reasonable interpretation within which to understand our experience.

---

45 Thomas Nagel, *The Last Word* (New York: Oxford University Press, 1997; 2001), 130, 130 n. 8.

Our observations of more complex realities emerging from their antecedents are quite understandable in the context of believing in God as Creator and Sustainer of the universe. If the universe is abundant in its evidence of an intelligence, mind, and purpose, this lends further reason to believe that our faith in God as Creator is based on what is fundamentally real about the world.

Mind and the Universe: Why Is the Universe Comprehensible?

"The eternal mystery of the world," said Albert Einstein, "is its comprehensibility."[46] The basis for any scientific thinking about the universe is that there is order and regularity in its working and that disciplined thought and observation can identify that order. Without this conviction and working faith, the whole scientific enterprise would be pointless and futile.

Mention of the regularity and order of the universe raises the question to any thoughtful observer: Why is it so? Why are there any laws at all? Astrophysicist Paul Davies asks why is there a set of laws that "drive the searing, featureless gases coughed out of the Big Bang toward life and consciousness and intelligence and cultural activities such as religion, art, mathematics and science?"[47] John Polkinghorne speaks of the "rational transparency" that

---

46 Albert Einstein, *Out of My Later Years*, rev. ed. (New York: Philosophical Library/Open Road, 2015), 64.

47 Paul Davies, in Krista Tippett, ed., *Einstein's God: Conversations about Science and the Human Spirit* (New York: Penguin Books, 2010), 35.

drives the scientific observer to wonder.[48] One potential response to this undeniable observation about the world is just to accept that that is "the way it is." But we can hardly avoid any effort to explain why and how the world can be ordered by laws whose precision and regularity make life possible.

A second aspect of this question is the matter to which we earlier referred: the emergence of mind from matter. We know that we and other creatures depend on a physical structure for our lives. But we also manifest the presence of mind, and our mental life cannot be reduced without remainder to the physical. We readily recognize the physical process that has brought us into being, but our experience of consciousness and thought cannot be dismissed as nothing but a physical process. Those who believe in God believe that there is evidence of intelligence and intention in the evolution of the world to its present state. We understand God as the Ultimate Knower, whose rational direction is observable in the continuing creation and sustenance of the world. It is a long-standing conviction that the Genesis reference (1:26) to God's creation of humans in God's own image is a reference to, among other qualities, the gift of a mind.

The truth of the matter is, as philosopher Philip Clayton puts it, "In us matter has become conscious of itself, of its history, and perhaps of its ultimate origins."[49] We are those, Clayton continues, who can reason about right and wrong, feel reverence toward

---

48 John Polkinghorne, "The Harmony of Science and Faith," in Francis Collins, ed., *Belief: Readings on the Reason for Faith* (New York: Harper, 2010), 209.
49 Philip Clayton, "Neuroscience, the Human Person, and God," in Ted Peters and Gaymon Bennett, eds., *Bridging Science and Religion* (Minneapolis: Fortress Press, 2003), 120.

the world, and hunger for immortality. In grasping and appreciating the beauty and consistency of the rational order of the world, we in the mind of many believers are catching a glimpse of the mind of God.

The fact that draws our attention and wonder is the apparent "cognitive fit" between disciplined minds and the very structure of the universe. Why is it that we assume our mental workings can have any power to understand the workings of the world around us? How can mathematics, a creation of the human mind, understand and predict how the universe works? We alluded earlier to the workings of British and French mathematicians who puzzled over the movements of Uranus. Its movements did not fit into the patterns that would be predicted for them to follow. From their calculations they concluded mathematically that there must be a planet hitherto unknown that was associated with Uranus. They specified where it should be located and sighted. In 1846 telescopes focused on the place predicted, and within an hour the planet now known as Neptune was discovered.[50] Why should there be such congruence between the calculations of human minds and the real workings of the universe?

For those who believe in God, the dawning of consciousness and thought is a reflection of the creative mind of God, whose own rational ordering of the world is the very basis for scientific understanding of the world. Believers readily interpret the capacity of the human mind to understand the workings of the world as an indication that we are created in God's image. The consonance between our minds and the universe is consistent with the

---

50 McGrath, *Surprised by Meaning*, 16 (see chap. 2, n. 5).

conviction that both we and the universe around us are created and sustained by God.

Moral Obligation: Is There a Foundation for Our Feeling of Ought?

Christian ethics has traditionally connected the sense of what we ought to do with the will of God. Religious believers have held that the outlines of God's will were embedded in Scripture and tradition. There can be no ethical or moral law, they have insisted, without a Supreme Being who is omniscient and infinite in goodness and whose will is rightfully binding upon all. Fydor Dostoyevsky's frequently quoted conclusion is: "Without God and the future life . . . everything is permitted, one can do anything."[51] To make this statement does not mean that atheists are less moral than believers, nor does it suggest that people who do not believe in God are bereft of moral feelings. The question is whether there is any foundation in reality for such feelings, or whether they are simply artifacts of our personal outlooks or creations of the society in which we live. Does my sense of obligation reflect a claim that has foundations deeper than my personal feelings and my social context?

Relativistic Explanations of Moral Obligation

It is clear that a sense of moral obligation widely persists in a secular era, even among those who do not believe that it is based on

---

51 Fyodor Dostoyevsky, *The Brothers Karamazov,* trans. Richard Pevear and Larissa Volokhonsky (New York: Farrar, Straus, and Giroux, 1990), 589.

the will of a Supreme Being. The secular mind faces a challenge to explain why this should be so. How is the secularist to counter Dostoyevsky's contention that without God everything is permitted?

Some attempt to account for our sense of moral obligation by regarding it simply as residue from our evolution as human beings. Our forebears who were self-sacrificial and loving, some argue, tended to survive at a higher rate than others. Richard Dawkins speculates that our sense of obligation for altruistic behavior emerges from: (1) care of the kinship group; (2) the prospect of reciprocity and payback from the kinship when we are in need; and (3) the benefit of cultivating a reputation and standing for being helpful to others by representing oneself as an individual with conspicuous generosity.

Perhaps some will protest that this really doesn't explain the urge to kindness and generosity by the moral giants among us, both known and unknown. Dawkins's explanation for any such generosity is that it is a "mistake," a blessed mistake, to be sure, but a mistake nonetheless. In more primitive times, he explains, we lived in close kinship patterns. This proximity with kinship groups programmed into us certain urges for altruism. Those urges have become habitual. When we no longer live in kinship groups, those urges "misfire" and prompt us to act with charity and generosity toward people outside our kinship group. Dawkins assures us that he doesn't mean to label acts of altruism as "misfiring" or "mistakes" in a pejorative sense. He indicates that he is just seeking to explain how they evolved in us. He thus avoids granting any status to value beyond our instincts and acquired patterns of conduct.[52]

---

52 Dawkins, *The God Delusion*, 219–21 (see chap. 7, n. 26).

Those who think in these terms note the wide disparities in the conduct that is commended or proscribed in different cultures. These differences prompt them to contend that moral laws are really quite arbitrary and depend for their standing not on divine decree or on human reason but on the sheer exercise of power. There is no way that an "ought" can arise out of a factual state of affairs, according to proponents of this view. Sociologist Philip Gorski, for example, describes supposed moral imperatives as mere illusions. Moral directives are largely derived from what was found useful by our society in the past. They may be discarded when they are no longer found to be useful in the present. That we feel that murder and rape are intrinsically wrong is to be attributed to the fact that these proscribed actions do not serve our particular interests.

These theories, and variations of them that appear from time to time, really do not explain moral obligation as we experience it. In their own ways these views reduce the sense of ought not to binding moral obligations but to a personal preference, blunt assertion, or coercion.

The Schizophrenia of Modern Morals

This decoupling of moral obligation from grounding in a reality transcending our personal or social situation has created what Tim Keller calls the "schizophrenia" in the morals of modernity. The division that Keller finds in some contemporary ethics originates in their insistence that moral obligations are mere personal or social preferences, "self-authorizing," to use Charles Taylor's term, and at the same time they claim that they are—or should be—binding upon all. Mari Ruti, a professor at the University of Toronto, puts it succinctly: "Although I believe that values are socially constructed rather than God given . . . I do not believe that gender inequality is any more defensible than racial inequality, despite repeated efforts to pass it off as culture-specific 'custom' rather than an instance of injustice."[53]

In other words, moral values are held to be constructions of a social group, yet claims based on those values are said to constitute an obligation for all. What, we should ask, does one culture create that another culture with equal authority could not revoke? On what basis should my personal or societal perceptions of obligation make a universal claim? Keller observes that in these relativistic views moral obligations can be heeded or laid aside as one chooses. Relativistic perspectives provide "no reason not to act in any way we desire, if we can get away from it practically. There's simply no way to tell right from wrong, so we shouldn't try."[54] And yet there is still an inclination—despite our theories to the contrary— to claim that certain moral obligations are binding for all.

Newspaper columnist David Brooks gives another example of the divided mind in our moral reasoning by referring to what intellectual historian Wilfred McClay has termed "the strange persistence of guilt." Brooks notes the erosion of certain religious and philosophical viewpoints that once grounded our sense of right and wrong. In the absence of these organizing worldviews, he writes that it would seem that we would settle into a nonjudgmental form of relativism. Everyone could follow a personal preference, and

---

53 Mari Ruti, *The Call of Character: Living a Life Worth Living* (New York: Columbia University Press, 2014), 36, quoted in Timothy Keller, *Making Sense of God: An Invitation to the Skeptical* (New York: Viking, 2016), 179–80.
54 Keller, *Making Sense of God*, 183.

no one should contest an individual's right to follow his or her own leading. But what we are observing, he points out, is quite the opposite. Society, he says, has become a "free-form demolition derby of moral confrontation." At town hall meetings and on college campuses there are head-to-head contests between competing moral views. We debate abortion, transgender bathrooms, the alt-right, and other issues of the day. As we have become more secular, and as overarching political ideologies have grown less dominant, Brooks holds, we have become ever more fervent in our moral crusades.

Our situation results in what we could term another form of schizophrenia: the persistence of guilt in the context of seeming relativism. We feel impelled to address issues of colonialism, slavery, poverty, water pollution, and many others. Wilfred McClay concludes that we have an "inextinguishable need to feel justified." We think in these religious categories, yet we have no theoretical framework or rituals to address our need for grace, forgiveness, and redemption. Lacking the notion of a loving universe and divine mercy, we seek to gain our innocence by assuming a role of a victim who is free from moral responsibility.[55]

We find ourselves, therefore, with a divided mind on the question of moral obligation. Even Philip Gorski, despite his theory that the feeling of moral obligation is merely an illusion, admits that few can really believe in this theory in actual practice. "Our own relativism is rarely as radical as [our] theory requires," he concedes. "Who would now deny that the Holocaust was evil?"[56]

---

55 David Brooks, "The Strange Persistence of Guilt," *New York Times*, March 31, 2017.
56 Keller, *Making Sense of God*, 183.

The Good and the True Ends for Human Life

We find some means for overcoming this schizophrenic predicament if we consider our moral obligation in relationship to the true *telos* or end of human life. Simply put, we know what is good for human beings—what is morally obliged—by evaluating possible conduct within the context of the purpose for which we exist. Alasdair MacIntyre expresses it in this way: "To say what someone ought to do is at one and the same time to say what course of action will in these circumstances as a matter of fact lead toward a man's [or a woman's] true end and to say what the law, ordained by God and comprehended by reason enjoins. Moral sentences are thus used within this framework to make claims which are true or false."[57] Thus MacIntyre holds that our sense of moral obligation is more than a personal preference. We know what is good or morally obliged for an individual by a prior understanding of the purpose for which he or she exists. If we call a watch "good," he suggests, we mean that it effectively serves its intended function of keeping time. Similarly, to speak of a farmer as good is to affirm that he or she serves effectively in producing food. The judgment that a watch or a farmer is good is dependent on a prior factual judgment about the appointed purpose or function of each. Where there is conviction about the purpose of human life, the concept of the good is not merely an individual feeling, therefore, or the construct of a particular social setting. It is a judgment based on what we hold to be the purpose of life.[58]

---

57 MacIntyre, *After Virtue*, 51 (see chap. 5, n. 6).
58 Ibid., 58–59.

Moral Obligations and Constructs of the World

Our discussion of the sense of moral obligation has therefore brought us to a set of stark alternatives. If the world is a self-created and self-explanatory entity, then the true end or purposes for the humans within it are whatever humans as individuals or societies designate them to be. If, on the other hand, the world is viewed as the creation of a gracious and loving God, there is a basis in the nature of things for discerning what is right and morally binding upon us.

We have stated throughout that our schema, our understanding of the world, is embedded in traditions and narratives. The Genesis accounts of the creation, for example, declare that the world issues forth from God and that human beings are accorded a special place in, and inherit a commensurate responsibility for, tending the creation of God. The account of the life, death, and resurrection of Jesus Christ narrates the manner in which God seeks to redeem human beings and restore a relationship with them. Becoming a Christian involves finding the story of our lives in that gospel narrative, for it is through that story that we understand our true end and goal. We are reminded of Alasdair MacIntyre's resistance to the idea that we create our own moral dispositions. "I can only answer the question of 'What am I to do?'" he insists, "if I can answer the prior question 'Of what story do I find myself a part?'" Every action is always an "episode," he says, "in a possible history."[59] It is through the narrative that we embrace the purpose for our living and conduct that is consistent with that purpose.

---

59 Ibid., 216.

The parable of the good Samaritan in Luke's Gospel illuminates this basis for moral obligation. When the lawyer asked Jesus what one must do to inherit eternal life, Jesus in turn questioned him about what his tradition said about the true end of life. The lawyer responded, "You shall love the Lord your God with all your heart, and with all your soul, and with all your strength, and with all your mind; and your neighbor as yourself." Jesus replied, "You have given the right answer; do this, and you will live" (10:27-28).

By his response Jesus clearly indicated that the true good for human life was in relationship—a consuming commitment to the love of God and wholehearted participation in a beloved community with one's fellow human beings.

But the lawyer pressed for more specification of what it means to love your neighbor as yourself. Jesus responded with a story. A man was assaulted on the road from Jerusalem to Jericho. He was robbed and left half dead. Two temple officials passed the victim on the roadside. Religious regulations required them to stay at least six feet from a dead body lest they become ritually defiled and thus be required to undergo a weeklong procedure of purification before they could resume their temple duties. Then a Samaritan man came down the road. He stopped, bound up the victim's wounds, and made provision for his care at a nearby inn. Having told the story, Jesus answered the lawyer's question with another question: "Which of these three, do you think, was a neighbor to the man who fell into the hands of robbers?" (v. 36).

The story Jesus chose was clearly selected to delineate moral obligation that transcended the societal and religious requirements of the day. People of the day speculated about whether the pro-visions of the Law required Jews to treat Romans, Syrians, and other non-Jews as neighbors. By selecting the Samaritan as a role model, Jesus showed clearly that certain moral obligations overrode the then prevailing social rules. He changed the question from an inquiry into how far the lawyer was obliged to extend the category of a neighbor into what conduct was befitting for one who loved his neighbor as himself. The Samaritan's conduct showed that a neighbor was anyone who stood in need.

We are reminded that the Samaritan was a hated adversary to the Jews. Their theological differences traced back to ancient disputes when the Samaritans were said to have associated with the heathen who had come into the land. Samaritans were forbidden to worship in the temple when the Jews returned from exile in 536 BCE, so Samaritans built their own temple on Mount Gerizim. Jews cursed the Samaritans in the synagogues and prayed that they would have no share in eternal life. Samaritans defiled the temple in Jerusalem by scattering men's bones in the temple area, making it impossible to celebrate the Passover.[60] This ancient enmity created a dilemma for the lawyer who asked the question. Instead of spelling out what was required, Jesus asked the lawyer to identify who in the story had faithfully lived out the purpose of loving his neighbor. The lawyer could not even bring himself to let the word *Samaritan* pass his lips. Instead, he said, "The one who showed him mercy." And Jesus said, "Go and do likewise" (v. 37).

The story Jesus told revealed a Samaritan whose act of compassion fit appropriately in a life directed toward loving his neighbor. All the prevailing social constructs—and doubtless his personal inclinations as well—would have excused the Samaritan from any

---

60 Fisher, *The Parables of Jesus*, 83–86 (see chap. 6, n. 27).

contact with the victim. The Samaritan's act was consonant with his purpose to love God and neighbor, and he was cited by Jesus as an exemplary neighbor to one in need. The sense of moral obligation for the Samaritan emanated from who he was created to be.

Our point in this discussion has been to show that even those who contend that morals are merely personal preferences or social constructions often imply that some obligations are binding upon all. Yet the relativist theory provides no basis for understanding why this should be so. Some will respond that heeding moral commitments is just a responsibility of being human. We certainly can affirm that this is true. But responsibility is a relational term. It implies a relationship with one with authority to hold us accountable. If moral obligation is merely a personal feeling or societal construction, there appears to be no basis for insisting that my sense of moral obligation has any rightful claim on the conduct of another.

One further note is needed. To speak as we have about universal claims is not to claim that there is universal agreement about the content of those claims. Obviously we cannot claim consensus on what is required of us—though, as we noted, it would be difficult to find anyone, whatever his or her theories, who would say a good word for the Holocaust! Individuals and societies will arrive at different conclusions on the nature of moral obligation, to be sure. Our contention, however, is that in making claims for our sense of moral obligation, our insistence that they are binding on others, we are implying a transcendent source of the good for which relativistic theories make no provision. If God has created life with intention and purpose, then it is not in the least surprising that there are intimations of moral obligation that are binding upon all. This is the reality to which I believe David Bentley Hart was alluding when he wrote, "It is certainly not the case that one needs to believe in God in any explicit way in order to be good; but it certainly *is* the case . . . that to seek the good is already to believe in God, whether one wishes to do so or not."[61]

Our point in the discussion is not to point to the presence of the sense of moral obligation as a proof for the existence of God. It is rather to hold that our faith in God leads us to believe that our sense of moral obligation is founded on the purpose and ends that human life was created to fulfill.

Conclusion

Our discussion in this and the previous chapter sought to show the consonance between our faith and trust in God and the nature of the world as we observe it. We have noted a series of statements related to remarkable aspects of our universe:

- the fact that there is anything at all;
- that creation appears to be an ongoing process and not a single event;
- that an extremely delicate combination of variables makes human life possible;
- that mind and consciousness emerged from matter;
- that these minds can comprehend the universe from which they emerged;
- that moral obligations appear to be founded on what we were created to be.

---

61 David Bentley Hart, *The Experience of God* (New Haven, CT: Yale University Press, 2013), 257–58.

Our contention throughout has been that these striking developments are understandable if the world, as we believe, is created and sustained by God. If our faith in God thus illuminates and helps explain otherwise inexplicable observations about our universe, we have reason to regard this as evidence for the validity of the faith in which we stand.

REFLECTION QUESTIONS

1. How do you respond to Lesslie Newbigin's contention that "we do not come to know anything except by believing something"? Can you think of illustrations of his point? Can you think of exceptions?

2. The author refers to six remarkable observations about the universe and suggests that belief in God provides a credible explanation of how the universe came to be as it is. Which of these observations in your mind are most vivid and persuasive? About which, if any, would you raise a question and have reservations?

3. How helpful is it in your estimation to use the analogy of the world as God's body? Is the analogy of the mind and its interaction with the body an apt parallel to God's transcendence and interaction with the world? How does the analogy fit, and how does it potentially mislead?

4. Do the notions of the big bang and creation as a process assist in understanding the affirmations about the creation in the Genesis accounts? Can the accounts of Genesis fit intelligibly with contemporary theories? Or is there a clash between the two?

5. Is the illustration of scattered Scrabble tiles and a line from Shakespeare an apt parallel to the apparent bias toward life in the universe? Does belief in God and divine intention help in understanding the apparent purpose in the created order?

6. Do you think that people generally wish for there to be a God? What would prompt an individual such as Thomas Nagel to want there not to be a God?

7. How can human minds and the mathematics they have created accurately understand and predict features in our universe that were hitherto unknown? What does that lead you to believe about the creation? About God? About humans?

Faith in Community

*They devoted themselves to the apostles' teaching and fellowship,
to the breaking of bread and the prayers.*

—Acts 2:42

This book is designated for those who want to learn about faith, whether vigilant believer or reluctant skeptic. In one way or another, those camps likely include us all. One aim in the discussion has been to show that some of the apparent blocks to Christian trust and belief in God for men and women in the past have disappeared and that new understandings of faith have emerged, creating new openings to help make authentic faith and trust in God a credible and urgent option. We have contended that the perspective of Christian faith sheds light and helps to make sense of the world as it is coming to be understood.

To whatever degree that case has been made, we must concede that the sense-making dimension of faith in God is only one aspect of how we know God. Knowing God entails an experience *of* God and not merely conclusions *about* God. Knowing God and faith in God require a way of relating our lives to the infinite mystery that encircles us. It involves awe, reverence, and devotion to the source of life, love, pardon, and hope in which our lives are rooted and to which they are entrusted at the last day.

Seeking Experience of God

There are several signs that many of our contemporaries are seeking earnest participation in faith and not merely speculation about faith. We will speak later of the "spiritual but not religious" phenomenon that is gaining in strength in the United States and elsewhere. Whatever our sentiments about this development, we can surely agree it displays an earnest desire to taste and feel the experience of God and not merely to debate whether God exists. More and more frequently we are hearing a statement about personal faith prefaced by the disclaimer, "I'm not really religious, but I have a real concern about . . ."

Theologian Harvey Cox sees convincing signs that we are entering what he terms an "Age of the Spirit." This age, he holds, brings with it a rapid growth of Christianity in areas other than the West. He believes that the emphasis of this emerging movement is upon spiritual experience and discipleship and that it is accompanied by diminished attention to creeds and hierarchies. This age, in Cox's view, follows the "Age of Belief," which lasted for about fifteen hundred years and the "Age of Faith" that began with Jesus and his disciples. That first age of the church focused on living in the Spirit of Jesus, embodying his hope for the kingdom, and following him in this work. This period characterized the Christian movement until the end of the third century, when Christianity became the official religion of the Roman Empire.[1] Then, according to Cox, the emphasis changed from faith *in* Jesus to doctrines *about* him. The coming "Age of the Spirit," in Cox's view, marks a time in which people are drawn more into the experiential elements of faith, placing less emphasis on doctrine and church organization.

Diana Butler Bass also holds that what is happening in our midst is the equivalent of another "Great Awakening," a movement that is quite comparable to other awakenings in American history. She sees evidence of this awakening, for example, in Pentecostal fervor, in the revival of spiritual practices, in the appearance of the "emergent" church, and in the growth of Christianity in the Global South. Bass outlines the dissolution of one era and the beginnings of a new awakening in the church in her book *Christianity after Religion: The End of Church and the Birth of a New Spiritual Awakening.* She also cites the rising number of those who identify themselves as "spiritual but not religious." In the United States 30 percent of adults identify themselves in this way. About 40 percent of Canadians and 51 percent of the British understand themselves in these terms. According to Pew Research, from 2007 to 2014 the number of people who identified themselves as both spiritual and religious grew from 52 percent to 59 percent. And people who consider themselves as not affiliated but feel a "deep sense of wonder about the universe at least weekly" rose from 38 percent in 2007 to 47 percent in 2014.[2]

---

1   Cox, *The Future of Faith*, 5 (see chap. 4, n. 8).

2   See David Masci and Michael Lipka, "Americans May Be Getting Less Religious, but Feelings of Spirituality Are on the Rise," *Fact Tank* (Pew blog), January 21, 2016, http://www.pewresearch.org/fact-tank/2016/01/21/americans -spirituality/.

It is not entirely clear, of course, what each person who designated himself or herself "spiritual but not religious" actually means by that category. To focus more upon meanings, Bass asked groups in several parts of the country to make word associations with each category. Some of the key words these groups associated with "spiritual" were: *experience, connection, transcendence, searching, intuition, prayer, inner life, and meditation.* On the other hand, the respondents associated the "religious" category with words such as *institution, organization, rules, order, dogma, authority, beliefs,* and *certainty.*[3]

> **Relational faith focuses on experiencing God rather than acquiring more information about God.**

The traditional terms we in the West have used for the last three hundred years in thinking about God have often been doctrinal and individual. Discussions of faith have sometimes centered on conclusions about a transcendent reality and how those conclusions could be defended or denied. It is in this context that some are suggesting that the issue is not so much *what* to believe but *how* to believe. However, putting the question of knowing God in an individual way fails to acknowledge that God is known not by detached individuals but in community with others. Faith is relational rather than exclusively or primarily informational. Relational faith focuses on experiencing God rather than merely acquiring more information about God.[4]

---

3 Diana Butler Bass, *Christianity After Religion: The End of Church and the Birth of a New Spiritual Awakening* (New York: HarperCollins, 2013), 56–57, 69, 92–93.

4 See this emphasis by Parker Palmer and Diana Butler Bass in her *Christianity after Religion,* 113–14.

In light of this, Bass believes that we need to reconsider the manner in which people come to faith and participate in the community of faith. We have often identified the first step in knowing God as declaring our agreement with doctrinal statements about God. We have sometimes made those public professions of faith more prominent than experiencing the reality of God. Following assent to these doctrines, the new believer was accepted into church membership. Thereafter he or she would be enjoined to follow the implications of baptism and church membership by engaging in acts of service to others, stewardship of time and money, and participation in public and private worship of God. This sequence was not stated or practiced in quite this wooden fashion, but it was implied in the manner in which we proceeded. We implicitly declared that knowing God was first a matter of getting straight on what we believed, then molding our conduct to the standards of our Christian profession, and then joining the church.

Diana Butler Bass suggests that we ought to consider reversing the order. We ought to think first of belonging to the community, then engaging in practices of the community, and then—on the basis of this firsthand experience—articulating the convictions of Christian faith. She puts it concisely: we should concentrate on "belonging, behaving, and believing."[5] She terms this the "great reversal." With this in mind, we look first at "belonging" and the matter of experiencing faith in community.

---

5   Bass, *Christianity After Religion,* 201ff.

Ministry on Rocky Ground

Sue D'Allesio was a student in the theological seminary where I served.[6] Sue had already begun her career as a professional musician when she sensed and responded to a call to Christian ministry. An excellent student, she delighted in the intellectual aspect of theological seminary and loved the discussion of abstract ideas. She also elected to undertake a part-time ministerial appointment while she continued her graduate professional studies.

The church to which Sue was assigned was no longer large enough to support a full-time pastor, and Sue was the latest in a series of students who drove ninety miles from the seminary to serve in the community on Sundays and every second Wednesday. Congregants felt that they were not good enough to deserve a full-time pastor, and they concluded that the denomination would not be concerned if the congregation were to close. The church was located in a poor community with a population of about four hundred. The church numbered about seventy-five members, but the Sunday morning congregation usually had only fifteen or twenty people in attendance. The community was seriously depressed. Factory workers were hit hard by a downturn in the economy. Alcoholism was evident, and drugs were sold under a large oak tree on Main Street. Houses and yards were littered and in bad repair. More than half of the townspeople lived with welfare assistance.

---

6   Sue has written a report and analysis of her ministerial service in "Farming on Rocky Ground," in *Faith and Ministry in Light of the Double Brain*, ed. James B. Ashbrook (Bristol, IN: Wyndham Hall Press, 1989), 107–23.

Little in Sue's middle-class experience and her academic studies prepared her for the blue-collar community in which she sought to serve. She began, however, carefully listening to the stories of the people in the town. They were what theologian Tex Sample has termed "hard-living" people.[7] They had to focus on immediate issues of survival and getting by, and there was little opening for long-range or abstract thinking. Sue learned to understand, respect, and love the people whose values, lifestyle, and means of expressing themselves were so different from her own. In her Sunday sermons she focused on concrete stories of the Bible that seemed to connect with the stories the people were telling her about their community and their church. She centered on biblical stories that suggested alternatives to their very low estimate of themselves and their community. She gave a great deal of attention to ways she could help the people see themselves, their church, and their community in a new light. The stories, she said, seemed to prompt imagination and hope among the people. She noted that the people began to find themselves in many of the Bible stories they heard from the pulpit.

As the people in the church talked about their congregation, the women in the church said that they wanted to attract more young (i.e., under sixty years old) women of the community. Sue asked them what was holding them back. They reported that they had made an effort to start a women's group eight years ago, but no one came. Sue focused on their desire to reach the younger women in town, and she helped two women of the congregation

---

7   Tex Sample, *Hard Living People & Mainstream Christians* (Nashville: Abingdon Press, 1993).

plan how they could start a group. Noting that some of the younger women they wanted to attract had daytime obligations, she helped the two leaders start a group that would meet in the evening. They identified programs that would relate to the needs of prospective members of the group. They agreed that women could join the group even if they were not church members.

After two meetings of the evening group, now called the Mustard Seeds, the women came to Sue with a problem. In response to their invitation to the whole community, a woman I will call Rebecca joined the group, and they implored the pastor to find a way to bar her from participating. They informed Sue that Rebecca wasn't the kind of person they had in mind for the group. But Sue questioned, "Didn't you want to attract members whether or not they were members of the church?" They responded that the pastor just didn't understand what Rebecca was like. They said that she was foul-mouthed, unwashed, and smelled offensive. "She," they informed Sue, "is no good."

Sue reminded them that their congregation existed to help people. God had given them an opportunity, she said, to reach out with love and care for people just as Jesus did. She asked them to show love and care for Rebecca, even if they didn't approve of her attire, her lack of personal hygiene, or her foul language. Though the leaders were reluctant, they started complimenting Rebecca whenever she made any attempts at grooming and controlling her language. They reported that Rebecca was asking a lot of questions about Jesus. They required that Rebecca clean up her language and refrain from smoking in church. They complimented her whenever she shampooed her hair or washed well before their meetings. Since Sue's schedule did not include nights the Mustard

Seeds met, she asked for Rebecca to come on Sunday to meet her. When she first met Rebecca, Rebecca was slumped in the back pew of the church. Sue was stunned by the offensiveness of even the "improving" Rebecca. Rebecca's hair was stringy, and her clothes looked like "rummage sale rejects." Her body smelled of cigarette smoke and sweat.

On one of the Sundays after Rebecca began attending, the morning service included a baptism. Rebecca informed the pastor that she didn't believe in baptism. She said, "I heard Jesus never baptized nobody. How come you do?" Then she left. But Rebecca returned to church early the next Sunday so she could see the children in the church school. When she asked if she could help, they put her in charge of taking attendance and putting the church school materials in order. She took up her new job with dedication. She started to issue attendance reports.

Each Sunday Rebecca, now a regular attendee, had a theological objection to raise with Sue. One Sunday, for example, her comment was that God wouldn't forgive a murderer. On another occasion she asked who thought up Advent. And she wanted to know why, if Jesus forgave us once, did we have to keep asking for forgiveness. Meantime, she read a booklet on how to work with preschool children and started leading this class in the church school. She even went to parents of preschoolers in town and told them they were wasting their kids' lives if they didn't send them to church school. She did love the children, and her class grew from five to seventeen in number. All the while her dress and grooming improved, and she now sat not in the back pew but in the middle of the congregation. She began associating more with the adults in the congregation, and she continued her preschool class.

To Sue's surprise Rebecca approached her about joining the church. She said that she knew she probably wasn't good enough, but she wondered how she could get baptized and join the church. On Pentecost Sunday, about a year after her first appearance at the church, Rebecca was baptized and became a member of the church. To a small circle of those in the church, she shared the story of her life. She confided that when she was six years old, she saw her father shoot her mother and then turn the gun on himself and take his own life. She had grown up in an orphanage where she had to fight to survive. She had later been in and out of foster homes. Her life had been a constant struggle, and she had never really had a family. No one in the community had known the course her life had taken until that day when she became a member of the church.

Rebecca was accepted for the person she was, and members of her circle came to see that it was their mission to love her and care for her as Jesus had cared for people. Through Bible stories and through membership in the group, she mattered to others and she mattered to God. Through the church, she came to see that she could help others as well. Rebecca's entrance into the faith involved a dynamic mixture of her background and a wistful searching for belonging and belief. While her story is hardly typical, there are elements or steps that illustrate that faith is appropriated in community.

Individualism and Community

Rebecca, no less than the rest of us, came to understand herself by her relationships—or lack of them—with other people. She had never had a family. Her parents were destroyed before her eyes when she was a child. All her associations had taught her that she was "no good," contemptible, unwanted, and unsightly. No doubt the circle of women to whom she disclosed her history represented the first family she had ever known. It was in a community centered in stories of faith that she came to know herself in a different way and patterned her life in a new direction.

Many have pointed out that there is a deep sentiment of individualism among Americans. There is of course much to commend a tradition of individual liberty, personal responsibility, and independence. But this tradition also has its limits. It may involve breaking away from family, community, and inherited ideas. In place of sustaining community, the tradition of individualism tends to stress autonomy, achievement through work, and association with others solely on the basis of shared individual interests. Cut off from history and community, such association as we enjoy may tend to become what sociologist Robert Bellah contemptuously termed "lifestyle enclaves."[8]

Bellah and his coauthors identified this individualism with a young nurse named Sheila who named her prevailing faith after herself. It was, she said, "Sheilaism." She affirmed that she believed in God, but she assured the researchers that she was not a "religious fanatic." She could not remember the last time she had attended a church. Sheila defined "Sheilaism" in these terms: "It's just try to love yourself and be gentle with yourself. You know, I guess, take care of each other. I think He would want us to take

---

8   Robert N. Bellah et al., *Habits of the Heart: Individualism and Commitment in American Life* (Berkeley: University of California Press, 1985), 154.

care of each other." And she was unwilling to identify anything much more specific about the tenets of "Sheilaism."[9]

Community and Narratives

However much we prize individualism, we have come to see that our identity is shaped in community. Alasdair MacIntyre suggests that the unifying identity of our lives is that of a character in a story. He emphasizes that we are "story-telling animals" and that we receive our identity according to the stories by which we live and by the communities of which we are a part. We evaluate the appropriateness of potential actions by their fit or lack of fit with the story of which we are a part. A prospective action is an "episode in a possible history" and evaluated as such. "I am," says MacIntyre, "what I may justifiably be taken by others to be in the course of living out a story that runs from my birth to my death."[10] That story, he adds, is embedded in communities of individuals through which I receive my identity.[11] The communities through which we identify ourselves are themselves bearers of traditions, inclusive narratives and reservoirs of understanding that have been shaped and reshaped over generations.

Participation in a community provides one with a narrative, a past, and a future that gives substance to the present. The power of a community's narrative was illustrated superbly by the role of the African-American churches in the civil rights movements in the 1960s and following. When Mrs. Rosa Parks refused to give

---

9   Ibid., 221.
10 MacIntyre, *After Virtue*, 217 (see chap. 5, n. 6).
11 Ibid., 221.

up her seat on the Montgomery bus on December 1, 1955, and risked arrest, harassment, job loss, and death threats, she was acting out of an identity conveyed by a tradition. Reportedly, a friend of Mrs. Parks, Mrs. Dorothy Height, asked her friend, "Rosa, what were you thinking when you sat there and refused to budge?" Mrs. Parks responded, "I had welling up within me the conviction that I was a child of God. And I knew that if I was a child of God, I couldn't take this humiliation one day longer." Her identity through a tradition of faith enabled her to defy the surroundings of segregation and act out of a contrasting identity.

Educator Parker Palmer, in commenting on Mrs. Parks's action, has noted that it is natural for people in a movement to find a place in what he terms a "community of congruence." Her understanding of herself as a child of God sprang from a tradition rooted in a community—the church. It was in that church that the story of God's liberating power was declared and embodied in ritual and song. Sharing that story in the community of the church fortified her will and vision so that she could hold it steadfastly in the midst of the public realm. The vision of freedom and justice fused in congruence with the larger story of God's action in Jesus Christ. The church, says Palmer, provided a place where the fragility of a vision and dream could be practiced and embraced.[12]

It was natural for a movement of people determined to be free to find in the biblical narrative a wider story that rooted and strengthened that movement. It was noteworthy that the movement for civil rights and dignity interpreted its vision, risk, suffering,

---

12 Parker J. Palmer, *The Courage to Teach* (San Francisco: Jossey-Bass, 1998), 172–73.

and victories in the language of the Bible. On the evening before his life was taken, Dr. Martin Luther King Jr. spoke of seeing the promised land from the "mountaintop." Whether he could walk with them into the promised land, he said, was in question, but there was no question that the people whom he led would arrive there someday. It was natural for Taylor Branch to organize the three volumes of his award-winning history of the civil rights movement around the narrative of the deliverance at the Red Sea and the vision of the promised land, entitling them *Parting the Waters, Pillar of Fire*, and *At Canaan's Edge*. People who risked everything in their determination to be free knew God in the context of a community that bore a story of God's deliverance in history.

The personal identities of those who led the civil rights movement were formed in the context of a community and not as solitary individuals. Personal identities are not created as solitary individuals. Rather, the personal narratives by which individuals live and by which their lives make sense are founded on a transcendent story. That transcendent narrative is found in the communities in which we participate.[13]

A Community Frame of Reference

Participation in a community of faith enables individuals to share a perspective on the world with others. The communal tradition becomes the lens through which the world is interpreted. We learn of God through a tradition, which is a reservoir of findings by our forebears as they have lived out their relationship with God. The

---

13 Grenz and Franke, *Beyond Foundationalism*, 82 (see chap. 8, n. 6).

biblical tradition spells out the way God may be known through recounting how God has been experienced in the past. The biblical tradition borne, proclaimed, and celebrated by the church is not a collection of infallible information. Rather, it is a record of "particularly transparent occasions," as John Polkinghorne puts it, that "have been open to an exceptional degree to the discernment of the divine will and purpose."[14] We come to learn who God is and what God wills through the testimony of traditions and stories that testify to what God has done in the past and what God promises for the future.

> Faith is a realm in which we dwell, a medium through which we move.

The proclamation of definitive occasions in which God's will and power are evident is the activity of a community of people, not a solitary venture. The gospel is proclaimed in a community of faith that finds its meaning and direction from the story. The narrative is studied, proclaimed, and symbolized in worship, prayer, and song. One's own life comes into focus as it is understood in the terms of the inclusive narrative. "To become a Christian involves learning the story of Israel and Jesus well enough to interpret and experience oneself and one's world in its terms."[15] When the story of one's life is understood in the context of the larger community's testimony of faith, then faith becomes not primarily a set of propositions held to be true but rather a realm in which we dwell, a medium through which we move. It becomes a

---

14 John Polkinghorne, *Theology in the Context of Science* (New Haven, CT: Yale University Press, 2009), 130.
15 Lindbeck, *The Nature of Doctrine*, 34 (see chap. 4, n. 11).

perspective on the world that is more and more taken for granted by members of the community. This does not mean that there are no disputes in interpreting the world. It is to say that disputes and arguments are conducted within the framework of a tradition and understanding. This very tradition itself, it should be noted, has been formed and refined by generations of the community of faith. Disputes are not devised to overthrow the basic picture of the world contained in the tradition. More often disputes center on the pertinence of the tradition to the present and the way it illuminates the current situation.

In the community of faith there is a fusion between one's life story and the tradition of the community. The story of faith becomes a dwelling in which we live and a vision by which we understand ourselves. Perhaps this is shown preeminently in Paul's affirmation to the Galatians: "I have been crucified with Christ; and it is no longer I who live, but it is Christ who lives in me" (2:19-20). And a parallel account was written to the Corinthians: "So if anyone is in Christ, there is a new creation: everything old has passed away; see, everything has become new!" (2 Corinthians 5:17).

Community and Experience

The Christian experience of the gifts of faith, of the forgiving and redeeming love of God, are gifts given to the whole community of faith and not to individuals alone. Individuals participate in these gifts as a function of sharing in the community of faith. It was in community that Rebecca came to see herself in a different manner and to know her standing before a loving God in a new way. In community we learn, through traditions developed over centuries, how our forebears experienced God. This places in us the expectation that the blessing of God's presence is a gift possible for us and leads us to the places where that presence has been found. It is far more typical for people to experience God's love and forgiveness in the context of a community and its collective story than as solitary and isolated individuals. The church's collective experience testifies to a reality that is available to all. It may be true, as theologian George Lindbeck insists, that "it is necessary to have the means for expressing an experience in order to have it."[16] At least we can say that the experience of God is opened to us in interaction with a living tradition through which God is known. It is often observed that the languages of people who live in arctic climates have several words denoting varying colors and consistencies for ice. Having access to these distinctions gives them the tools by which they interpret the ice and know what ice may be traversed and what may not.

There is some confirmation of the importance of the community in Christian experience from the Christian churches in Russia. In a visit with Russian Christians about a decade after the fall of the Soviet Union, I heard the story of adjustments they faced after seventy years or so during which the government had been officially atheistic. The Soviet government had taken elaborate steps to ensure that religious expressions would not reappear among the people and that university students would be instructed in atheistic orthodoxy. Theological terms such as *grace*, *forgiveness*, and *redemption* (or at least the theological nuances of those terms) were excised from the dictionaries. The only people

---

16 Ibid., 37.

who were encouraged to study theology were official professors of atheism, who were instructed to study church history and theology to demonstrate to properly orthodox atheists just how wrong the theologians were and how incorrect it was to have anything to do with religion. During those years religious experience survived primarily or solely in traditions around religious holidays or in rites such as baptism. Soviet authorities provided certain acceptable substitutes for religious rites, but particularly in rural areas the religious practices from previous generations persisted at least in some form.

As the prohibitions of most religious practices were lifted, however, many Russians found themselves without the language of belief. Books on religion had not been published during those seventy years, and many who wanted to study religion again were bereft of the language necessary to express it. To their delight, it was the professors appointed to teach atheism, those schooled in ways to eliminate religious expression, who could provide the religious terms by which it could be studied anew in a new context. It was the newly identified language of belief that helped them recognize and identify the stirring and flow of experiences and express them in intelligible and communicable faith. It is in the community of faith that we gain the language and stories that provide focus and context for experiencing the presence of God.

Community and Discernment

Once Copernicus had persuaded students of the stars that the sun rather than the earth was the center of our immediate neighborhood in the universe, they gathered in communities that employed that view in studying the motion of the heavenly bodies. In a sense, this new view of the sun as the center of our system was the world in which they dwelt. Their practice was governed by this perspective. In a similar sense, knowing God involves an ability to interpret or discern the world as an arena created and sustained by God. The gospel account provides a new set of first principles, a new schema of the world. Paul, as we have seen, proclaims that being "in Christ" places us in this new world. The old has passed away, and everything has become new (2 Corinthians 5:17). Paul wrote to the Romans: "Do not be conformed to this world, but be transformed by the renewing of your minds, so that you may discern what is the will of God—what is good and acceptable and perfect" (12:2).

Discerning the world as God's creation is a *communal* undertaking and not solely a solitary one. Sociologists stress the importance of conversation with others in maintaining a certain view of the world. It is not merely, they say, that the social groups of which we are a part are persistently defining the world. It is that in conversation with the groups of which we are a part we silently take for granted certain views of the nature of the world and how one interacts with it.[17] Without necessarily recognizing what is happening, we come to regard the world according to certain "plausibility systems" that are assumed by those with whom we affiliate.

A study in a university experimental psychology laboratory showed quite vividly how plausibility systems cause us to view the world in certain ways. A student was brought into a room with

---

17 See Peter L. Berger and Thomas Luckmann, *The Social Construction of Reality: A Treatise in the Sociology of Knowledge* (Garden City, NY: Doubleday, 1966), 152.

eleven other students and was told that he was to take part in an experiment on auditory acuity. He, along with the other eleven who were presumed also to be subjects, was asked simply to report to the host how many sounds were heard from a buzzer in the room. The student was the last one to register his answer. In the first sequence, he clearly counted four buzzes. However, to his amazement, every one of the first eleven who reported their count said there were five. The subject thought he must have been nervous and made a mistake, so when he was called on, he modified his count to five. On the next round he carefully counted nine sounds, but on this round as well, the first eleven reported that they had heard seven sounds. Our subject was thoroughly puzzled. After several rounds of this variance between his count and the unanimous count of the first eleven, he concluded that he need not count at all. The others surely knew what they were doing, and he simply concurred with whatever report the others gave, no matter how wildly their reports differed from what he thought he had heard.

Perhaps you have already guessed what was going on. The first eleven were not subjects at all. They were a part of the experimental design. The experiment was not set up to test accuracy in hearing. It was designed to see how aberrant the reports of the first eleven would have to be before our subject dared to differ. Their answer was that he was thoroughly taken in by the apparent consensus of those whom he supposed to be "in the know," and he simply responded as they had.

The subject in the experiment, while perhaps extremely compliant with group opinion, nonetheless illustrates the influence of communal settings on how we perceive the world around us. Saint

Paul urges us not to be conformed to the prevailing plausibility systems of the world but to be transformed by the renewal of our minds. The community of faith commends and proclaims a story of God's dealings with the world. Before we are taught what to do, we are instructed in how we are to see the way the world really is. The world in which God reigns—the kingdom of God—we are told, is a world in which those who mourn will be comforted, those who are merciful will receive mercy, and those who are persecuted will inherit the kingdom of heaven (Matthew 5:4, 7, 10). "What will it profit them," Jesus asks, "if they gain the whole world but forfeit their life?" (16:26). The parables offer metaphors from everyday experience to illustrate the reality of the world in the reign of God. Therefore, just as it is understandable that a father would rejoice when a renegade son has returned home, so it is natural that God welcomes sinners into the kingdom of God. "But we had to celebrate and rejoice," the father insists to an older brother, "because this brother of yours was dead and has come to life; he was lost and has been found" (Luke 15:32).

The communities of which we are a part have their own plausibility systems by which they understand life. They have their own codes for what constitutes success, what we should strive for, and who has superior standing. The man who had earned more than he could ever need but nonetheless kept on accumulating wealth said it well when he explained, "Life is a game. Money is how we keep score." A cartoon showed a man extensively intubated and obviously on his deathbed who said to a son sitting at his bedside, "I should have bought more stuff." Saint Paul urges us not to be conformed to the interpretive schemes of the world but to be "transformed by the renewing of your minds, so that you may discern what is the will of God—what is good and acceptable and perfect" (Romans 12:2).

{ **Faith is a communal undertaking.** }

It is true that faith must be appropriated personally and individually, but we deceive ourselves if we do not also view faith as a communal undertaking. In the community of faith, we practice viewing the world in the light of the narrative of faith. We join with others in declaring in our communal worship that God alone is to receive our ultimate loyalty and praise. All the lesser centers of value are at least secondary and less than ultimate. In this community of faith, we assume that the earth is the Lord's and that we are responsible to God for the care of it. We learn that God is close to the poor and the brokenhearted and makes their cause the cause of the divine. And we learn to see the world through the lenses of God's saving purposes. It is a communal undertaking.

A communal context is necessary, I suggest, both for maintaining a view of the world in which we seek to stand and for adopting a transformed view of that world. Again quoting Saint Paul, whose worldview was dramatically transformed, "So if anyone is in Christ, there is a new creation; everything old has passed away; see, everything has become new!" (2 Corinthians 5:17). When individuals overcome addiction, a part of their recovery is adapting their lives to a new world. They have been accustomed to accounting for their problems according to an old scheme. Recovery requires a reconstruction of their world. Sociologists Peter Berger and Thomas Luckmann, using the example of Paul's conversion from Saul, the persecutor of the church, say that an initial conversion is not the essential point. The issue is continuing in that conversion and embracing a new view of the world. Paul could *remain* Paul, they said, and not revert to the former Saul, "only in the context of the Christian community that recognized him as such and confirmed 'the new being' in which he located this identity. . . . The plausibility structure must become the individual's world, displacing all other worlds, especially the world the individual 'inhabited' before his alteration."[18]

Interpreting the Self and the World

Roberta Bondi, a church historian, reported in one of her writings that she felt she came face-to-face with God through the words of a fifth-century monk in his meditations for the brothers of the order. In this meditation the monks were admonished not to criticize one another but to treat them with the gentleness of God, "who especially loves the ones the world despises, and who is always so much more willing than human beings to make allowances for sin, because it is God alone who sees the whole of who we are and who we have been, who understands the depths of our temptations and the extent of our suffering."[19]

Bondi described the release she felt from the recognition that being rational was seeing the world through the eyes of God. And God sees the world through the eyes of love. We, too, she came to see, are invited to look at the world through the eyes of love.[20]

---

18   Ibid., 158.
19   Roberta C. Bondi, *Memories of God* (Nashville: Abingdon Press, 1995), 71.
20   Ibid., 77.

God, she realized, was not a tyrant who enforced the rules, but the One who sees us with understanding, love, and forgiveness. Adoption of Christian faith enables us to view the world with love and forgiveness.

> The Christian faith enables us to view the world with love and forgiveness.

Hearing and studying the stories of faith in the community helps us understand what is happening in the world. "To become a Christian," says theologian George Lindbeck, "involves learning the story of Israel and of Jesus well enough to interpret and experience oneself and one's world on its terms."[21] And this happens in the community of faith. The aim is not so much to "find ourselves" in the Bible but to allow the Bible's story to become our story and to shape the way we view our world. What does the world look like if Jesus is Lord? How does this mold our outlook on the world and our action within it?

We saw this principle at work in the parish led by Sue, the student pastor. The women of the church wanted other women in the community to join them. When the disreputable and quarrelsome Rebecca joined the group, the women wanted to find a way to exclude her, lest she drive other people away. With their pastor's help, they came to see that they had an opportunity to see the world and other people the way God sees them. So they, with reluctance, reached out to Rebecca. And Rebecca came to know herself and express herself according to a new narrative. Because of her trauma and rejection, she had never thought of herself as

---

21 Lindbeck, *The Nature of Doctrine*, 34 (see chap. 4, n. 11).

worthy. In community she came to understand herself in a new context and became a new person.

Conclusion

This chapter has focused on the conviction that we come to know God in community with others. Dorotheos of Gaza, from the sixth century, preached to the monks in his monastery that they were obliged to be understanding with one another even when the behavior of another was irritating. To illustrate this point, he drew a circle with God in the center and individual believers as points on the circumference of the circle. Then he drew lines from each individual on the circumference to God in the center. He suggested that there is no way to draw near to God without coming closer to other people.[22]

Both in sociology and in theology we are learning that we do not name or interpret the world as individuals. We live in a world of language and stories, and through them we discover who we are and comprehend the world in which we live. Yet in the midst of these understandings, there is an inclination to designate the world of faith as the realm of the subjective. This avoids controversy. We properly accord each person the right to entertain whatever views he or she desires. But religion that is treated solely as a private matter can claim no pertinence beyond the subjective self in which it dwells. We learn to know God not primarily as isolates but in community with others who embody a tradition in which God has become known.

––––––––––––––––––

22 Bondi, *Memories of God*, 201.

REFLECTION QUESTIONS

1. What do the words *spiritual* and *religious* mean to you? Are you more inclined to one than the other? Or do you embrace them both? If you identify strongly with one of the two, what questions would you raise with the person who makes the opposite choice?

2. How do you respond to Diana Butler Bass's suggestion of a "great reversal" in the way we come to faith? Is "belonging, behaving, and believing" the order in which most embrace Christian faith? Or may a person take the first step in faith through any one of the three? What is true of your own experience?

3. Can you identify any stories that help shape the person you understand yourself to be? Can you identify the stories by which others identify themselves? What biblical story is most important for your understanding of yourself and the decisions you must make?

4. Do you agree with the suggestion that becoming a Christian is embracing the Christian story as the narrative of your life? In this connection, how do you understand the apostle Paul's statement that those who are "in Christ" live in a new world? (2 Corinthians 5:17).

5. How typical do you believe the subject in the university psychology laboratory was in responding as he did? Is the tendency to conform amplified by where we live, those with whom we socialize, the news sources we select, or the activities or organizations in which we participate?

6. Marketing firms, advertisers, political organizations, and other groups can profile each of us by our individual age, gender, home location, economic status, purchasing patterns, and so forth. Does our participation in a community of faith in any way cause us not to conform to these indicators?

Faith in Action

As Jesus was walking along,
he saw a man called Matthew sitting at the tax booth;
and he said to him, "'Follow me."
And he got up and followed him.

—Matthew 9:9

Only those who believe obey . . .
and only those who obey believe.

—Dietrich Bonhoeffer,
The Cost of Discipleship

A crowd gathered on the city street, craning their necks to catch a glimpse of the famous circus performer as he walked on a wire stretched between two tall city buildings. After this performance, he took a wheelbarrow and called to the crowds, "Do you think I can push this wheelbarrow across the wire?" The crowds responded, "Yes, we believe." He immediately rolled the wheelbarrow across the wire. He then turned again to the amazed crowd below and asked: "Do you think I can roll a man in this wheelbarrow across the wire?" Once again the crowd shouted, "Yes, we believe." He then asked, "Who wants to volunteer?" No one from the crowd stepped forward.[1]

Perhaps this is a dramatic way of contending that faith and action are wedded in one response. German pastor and theologian Dietrich Bonhoeffer held the two to be indissoluble. In Levi's decision to heed Jesus's call and leave his tax booth (Matthew 9:9; Mark 2:14) or in Peter's response to step out in the storming waters at Jesus's call (Matthew 14:28-29), the act of believing and obeying were one. In acting, Levi and Peter manifested their belief and trust in Jesus.

In recent years research associated with Andre Ericson at the University of Colorado and the writing of Malcolm Gladwell have indicated that elite performers of any skill become proficient by practicing a minimum of ten thousand hours over a period of at least ten years. This calculation may be debatable, but it illustrates the investment required, even by the highly talented performer, to arrive at the highest level.

When we think of practice in the life of the Christian community as a means of knowing God, we are, of course, not thinking in terms of virtuoso performances. Christian living grows out of the basic biblical story that the Christian community interprets about what constitutes right action and right relationship in the world. We have seen that we come to know God through the story of how God disclosed the divine presence and will to those who have gone before us. The story of God's actions forms a way of

---

1   Robert G. Tuttle Jr., *Shortening the Leap: From Honest Doubt to Enduring Faith* (Anderson, IN: Bristol House, 2007), 154–55.

regarding the world, a perspective on the "way things are." In this sense one who knows oneself and the world through the lenses of the Christian story lives in a different world. A person of Christian faith knows the world as it has been created and redeemed by God because this God is disclosed in Jesus Christ.

It is instructive to remember how this approach to the world was sustained in the first two and a half centuries of the Christian movement. Christians were first known, as we have seen, simply as people of "the Way" (see Acts 18:26; 19; 24:14-23). The representatives of the Pharisees sent to Jesus acknowledged that Jesus taught "the way of God in accordance with truth" (Matthew 22:16). He was said to be the one who guided any who would follow "into the way of peace" (Luke 1:79). Before there were any doctrines or creeds about the identity and role of Jesus, there was the direct affirmation "Jesus Christ is Lord." This was not a matter of doctrine to which one gave assent as much as it was, as Harvey Cox has called it, a "pledge of allegiance." By that pledge followers of the Way declared loyalty to Jesus Christ and the priority of loyalty to his Way rather than to Caesar, who also claimed to be Lord.[2] What bound these early Christian communities together were not doctrines but patterns of living and following Jesus. Thus, these early faith communities centered their lives on sharing the Lord's Supper, praying, anticipating God's coming reign, and putting the Way of Jesus into practice. They experienced the presence of God's Spirit as together they took concrete steps in following Jesus's Way. It is true that doctrinal disputes required the church to adopt certain creedal standards by the fourth century,

---

2   Cox, *The Future of Faith*, 77 (see chap. 4, n. 8).

but in earlier epochs of Christian history, it was loyalty to following the Way of Jesus that guided the church in its expansion throughout the Mediterranean world.

Practices

The idea of Christian practice is of course not new. As followers of the Way, they imitated Jesus's ministry, which brought them closer to the loving and redemptive actions of God. While certain practices are particularly identified with the Christian community, the notion of "practice" is also used in society as a whole. We customarily use the term in describing certain professional or vocational groups. We speak of the practice of a physician or a lawyer. We acknowledge the practice of certain trades, such as carpentry. In carpentry one must master certain skills that are intrinsic to the craft (fitting joints, building walls that are square and plumb, and so on). A professional baseball player acquires certain skills, such as batting, throwing, baserunning, and fielding, and utilizes them in the practice of baseball. A musician rehearses the scales, fingering, and proper bodily stance as part of the practice of producing music.

In this general sense, practices are defined as "shared activities that are not undertaken as means to an end but are ethically good in themselves. . . . A genuine community—whether a marriage, a university, or a whole society—is constituted by such practices."[3] A general characteristic of any practice, as this definition describes,

---

3 Robert N. Bellah et al., *Habits of the Heart* (Berkeley: University of California Press, 1985), 335.

is that it is worth doing for its own sake. Alasdair MacIntyre uses as an example the experience of a child learning to play chess. A very able child even at age seven can learn some of the basic rules of the game. He or she may be prompted to take up the game by an ardent chess player. As an incentive, the child may be promised a bag of candy for completing each game. But if the instruction is successful, there will come a time when the child will no longer play for the external reward. The child's reward, as his or her proficiency grows, will no longer be external to the game. The reward for the child who grows in mastery of the game will come by gaining the analytical skills, the strategic imagination, and the sheer excellence that pertains to knowing the game and performing artfully and skillfully in it.[4]

The general notion of practice is not only an activity that is worthwhile for its own sake. It is also an activity that employs principles and rules of which the practitioner may be unaware. The chemist and science philosopher Michael Polanyi ventures that most bicycle riders are likely not aware of the principles that enable them to ride on a two-wheeled conveyance. He observes that when bikers begin to fall to the right, they turn the handlebars to the right so that the bicycle curves to the right. The result is that the centrifugal forces pushes cyclists to the left and offsets the forces that are pulling them in the opposite direction. Cyclists who begin to fall to the left follow the opposite procedure. Those setting out to ride a bike would not need to contemplate the theory of centrifugal force. Nor would they

---

4 MacIntyre, *After Virtue*, 188 (see chap. 5, n. 6).

need to calculate the angle of unbalance and its inverse rela-tionship to the square of the motion forward.[5] They would be instructed in how to sit on the bike saddle, how to push off with a foot, how to hold the handlebars. The practice of bike riding can employ a number of principles and ratios of which cyclists are unaware.

Similarly, most baseball pitchers seeking to learn and perform the practice of pitching do not prepare to throw a curveball by studying Bernoulli's principle describing the behavior of fluids and gases under varying pressures. They are instructed, rather, on how to hold the ball, how to utilize the body in throwing, and how to rotate the ball in the proper way. If they perform these actions skillfully, they may find success in throwing an effective curveball in the practice of baseball. What they may or may not know is that the principle named for Swiss physicist Daniel Bernoulli (1700–1782) explains how the rotation of the baseball, combined with the force of its motion toward home plate, creates a disparity of air pressure on both sides of the ball and causes the baseball to curve as it approaches the plate.

One characteristic of a practice, then, in addition to its intrin-sic value, is that it enables us to know more than we can explain. We can accomplish practices that we cannot put into words. Polanyi calls this knowledge, knowing more than we can say, "tacit knowl-edge." Tacit or implicit knowledge, as we have seen in practices, is confidence in and cooperation with forces and factors that we have not—and perhaps cannot—explain. Or, put another way, we can do more than we can say.

---

5   Polanyi, *Personal Knowledge*, 49–50 (see chap. 7, n. 15).

Christian Practices

We conventionally think that we come to know God by adopting certain doctrines or propositions about God. Knowledge of God in this context becomes a motion of the mind, an act of the intellect—or will—to conform to a certain verbal formula about God. Our best thinking about God and God's action in the world is certainly important. In the first instance, however, we may grasp more fully how we come to know God by considering the practices that promise to bring us into contact with the divine. Christian practices are embedded in the narratives and traditions through which the community of faith identifies who God is and how God works in the world. Throughout our discussion we have held that we come to know God through events that are particularly transparent to the divine presence. Through identifying and narrating these events, we come into contact with what we have called a "reservoir of understanding" in the experience of our faith community. Through these events the nature of God takes shape in the mind and imagination of the faith community. For the Christian church these events that disclose the divine presence among us center and find their focus in the life, death, and resurrection of Jesus Christ. Seeing the world through the perspective of the Christian story helps direct us to disclosures of God's will and God's doings in our world.

In short, events in the Christian story disclose to us what is fundamentally real. They become our lenses for interpreting and understanding the world. In them we are dealing with the Final Reality of our lives. By interpreting the world through the Christian gospel, we come to expect to find God's presence, God's love, grace, and redemptive work, in certain actions and practices. Since the events centering in Jesus Christ are identified as the focus and central acts by which God is known among us, we give special emphasis to those acts of faith, service, and devotion that are manifest in Jesus's life. Once again, as we imitate Christ, we can be assured that we are meeting the reality of God.

When we speak of Christian practices, therefore, we are speaking of acts, "channels of grace," through which Christians feel the presence of God at work in their experience. Acting and believing are essentially one event in faith. It is not so much that we have faith and then act it out. Rather, we hold that the action involved in Christian practice is a means by which the faith is grasped, experienced, and shared. Sometimes thought of as an alien obligation that must be fulfilled to please God, these practices are channels of grace, apertures in our lives through which we experience God's presence. Some have referred to them as "habitations of the Spirit."

What then are those practices we specifically identity as Christian? A list of all of them would, of course, be beyond the scope of this discussion. However, we can identify some types of practices that are embedded in Christian tradition, and these illustrate the realm of activities that we particularly designate as Christian.[6]

Personal and Community Worship and Prayer: Joining with others to hear the Word, to open our lives to the presence of God, to declare the praise of God, and to participate in the sacraments.

---

6   From many lists that might be cited, this is adapted from one that Craig Dykstra has developed utilizing many traditions within the Christian community. See his *Growing in the Life of Faith: Education and Christian Practices*, 2nd ed. (Louisville: Westminster John Knox Press, 2005), 42–43.

Prayer and personal praise and prayers for others. Meditation and openness to God.

Participation in Christian Community: Reading and studying the Bible and other writings, interpreting events in the world and daily events from the perspective of faith, testifying to God's presence to one another, sharing joys and sorrows, asking forgiveness and offering forgiveness, overcoming alienation with reconciliation.

Personal Relationships: Working in one's community to overcome alienation, extending hospitality and friendship to vulnerable and alienated individuals and communities.

Acts of Service and Reconciliation: Use of personal and community resources to address situations of need, providing personal assistance for people in crisis and continuing need, assisting in overcoming community ruptures and disputes.

Advocacy and Action for Just Structures in Society: Participating as a community member and citizen in overcoming structures of oppression and injustice, advocating for community and government laws and institutions that provide for and sustain just relationships among communities.

Action and Belief

The practices of Christian faith find their roots in a distinctive perspective on what the world is truly like. At the beginning of the Sermon on the Mount (Matthew 5–7), Jesus set forth what the world looks like when viewed through the coming kingdom of God. This vision contrasts with conventional views of the world. When God reigns, said Jesus, the very ones who appear to be crushed by the world—the poor in spirit, the mourners, the meek, the hungry—are the ones who are blessed. Indeed, the meek will inherit the earth, and the peacemakers, not the conquerors, will be called children of God. The Beatitudes, as we have seen, are instructions on how to see the world.

In the light of the coming kingdom that Jesus announced and embodied there are certain practices that help us experience the force of reality of God's reign, even while we wait for its full appearing. It is striking how practical Jesus was as he outlined appropriate responses. He did not dwell on theory. Rather, he outlined what concrete steps are in order, what acts will enable us to participate in the kingdom. Be reconciled to your brother or sister (Matthew 5:24). Do not resist an evildoer (v. 39). Love your enemies (v. 44). Contribute aid to others without calling attention to your generosity (6:3). When you pray, go into your room and shut the door and talk to God (v. 6). Avoid the display of your piety. Do not pile up empty phrases when praying (v. 7). Then Jesus not only suggested where and how to pray, but he gave an example of what to say (vv. 9-13). Jesus held that we believe in and experience the contours of the coming kingdom or reign of God through these concrete practices.

In this reading of the Sermon on the Mount, as well as other aspects of Jesus's teaching, the decision to act in the light of the kingdom is interrelated to one's belief and trust in its coming. Jesus implied that we experience God's reconciling love, forgiveness, and grace as *we* participate in acts that embody the kingdom. Dietrich Bonhoeffer, preaching and writing as a Christian resisting Nazism, stressed the unity of belief and obedience. Describing Peter following Jesus's call to step out of the boat and walk to him across the churning waters of the stormy sea,

Bonhoeffer said that stepping out of the boat *was* Peter's belief. We cannot claim to have faith, Bonhoeffer continued, so long as we fail to take the first step. "If you believe," he wrote, "take the first step, it leads to Christ."[7]

The first step in knowing God for many may well involve participating in a Christian practice. Food Pantry founder and director Sara Miles tells her own story of coming to faith. She was a totally "unchurched" woman in San Francisco and a single parent when she, on a whim, stepped into St. Gregory's Episcopal Church one Sunday morning. When they served Communion, she stepped forward with members of the parish and received the elements. She was surprised by her response. She had never had much patience with ritual and the liturgy. But as she found herself before the Communion table, she said she felt a surge of acceptance and belonging. She felt drawn to return.

Miles had worked in restaurants to support herself and her child, and she liked feeding people. She soon was participating in the food shelf run by the church and was intrigued that the table used for Communion also held the food items distributed to the people who came through the week to get food. The symbolic meal at Communion merged in her mind with the food that was given during the week to the people who needed it. She wasn't able to start with a concept of God, she said, and she couldn't argue philosophically about the existence of God. It was the "materiality" of Christianity, she said, that fascinated her. What held her imagination was "the compelling story of incarnation in

---

7   Dietrich Bonhoeffer, *The Cost of Discipleship*, 1st Touchstone ed., (New York: Touchstone, 1995), 67.

its grungiest details, the promise that words and flesh were deeply, deeply connected."[8]

As the ministry of the food shelf expanded, Miles began connecting the work of distributing food from the Communion table to the preaching of the Word. "It turned out," she said, "that the preaching of the Word . . . would be not only as satisfying as writing but almost as much fun as cooking for people." Instead of telling people to eat the "right" kinds of foods, she said that she was serving up words out of the lectionary. "'Here,' I was saying, as I salted and spiced a section of Scripture for the people at the early morning service, 'try this. It's so good, it's going to be the best thing you've ever tasted.'"[9]

Tacit Knowledge of God

Earlier I referred to the knowledge we rely on but cannot put into words. I noted that in mastering skills such as riding a bike or pitching a baseball, we concentrate first on the mastery of the skill and not, in the first instance, on the theory of how it works. We rely on forces and theories that we cannot at the time articulate. Earlier in the discussion I noted that Michael Polanyi termed what we know in this practical manner as tacit knowledge. He reminded us, in short, that we know more than we can say.

Perhaps there is a parable here for our knowledge of God. Even in our knowledge of other people, there are elements that we can rely on with full trust without being able to find theories

---

8   Sara Miles, *Take This Bread: A Radical Conversion* (New York: Ballantine Books, 2007), 70–71.

9   Ibid., 177.

that would explain them. We rely on the integrity, the skill, or even the love of another person in a manner that we cannot define by any equation or fact. We learn through interaction with that person who he or she is at the core, but we could never provide a diagram to show why that person is trusted and loved. Certain concrete acts of friendship and love help us express confidence in and depend on that person.

If this is true of other individuals, how much more is it true that people of faith learn to trust and rely on Ultimate Reality, God, in a manner that cannot be reduced to a formula or equation? It is not amiss to suggest that Christian practices represent ways that we experience, have access to, and rely upon the reality of God that we could never demonstrate in a mathematical calculation. If God is known in acts of mercy, justice, forgiveness, and reconciling love, then the practices that embody these values help us experience the reality of God, who is their Source.

A simple illustration of how we know God in practices took place in that most typical of congregational undertakings, a church supper. A congregation hosted a free community meal at the end of each month, a time when many people had already spent their monthly checks. One of the church's volunteer workers was washing cooking utensils in the church kitchen when one of the guests left the dining room and approached her. Her dress and grooming resembled that of any middle-class woman in her forties. She approached the volunteer and told her how much she appreciated the meal and how good the food had tasted. Then she added quietly, "You know, had it not been for this supper, I wouldn't have had anything to eat tonight." In that moment the grace and mercy of God registered with more acuity than it ever had before. The church volunteer, a woman from comfortable circumstances, sensed that she was participating in something much larger than herself, and the meaning of God as merciful, loving, and just became more than a casual phrase. Neither she nor any of the other volunteer workers on the supper had a convenient formula or equation to describe the love of God. On that evening they experienced more about what it meant than they could put into words.

Dr. Francis Collins is director of the National Institutes of Health. Before presidential appointment to this post, he, as a leading geneticist, was head of the Human Genome Project. This team successfully mapped the human genome, an enormously complex combination of genetic information that would reportedly fill sixty-six sets of *Encyclopedia Britannica*. The project has helped discover genetic "misspellings" that cause a number of genetic diseases and has provided an opening for changes in the sequencing of genes that hold the promise of preventing such diseases in the future.

When Dr. Collins had nearly completed his PhD in physical chemistry at Yale, he enrolled in a class in biochemistry. He was enthralled by his study of DNA and was fascinated with the possibilities of splicing different DNA fragments to prevent disease and work for human benefit. With this in mind he transferred to medical school at the University of North Carolina. As a medical student, he interacted with patients and was moved by the confidences they shared as he pursued his work as a healer. What particularly impressed him, he said, was the spiritual aspect of what some of his patients were experiencing. He noted the quiet confidence of some of his patients whose faith assured them of the ultimate peace of God's care in life and in death. Collins reported that he came to his medical practice an atheist, and to that point he was prone to dismiss religious faith and trust in God as a psychological crutch or a thin cultural accretion. Yet he could not deny the peace and courage that his patients gained from their rootage in prayer and faith. If their faith were only a crutch, why did his patients demonstrate such strength in confronting illness, disability, or death?

In what Dr. Collins has described as his most awkward moment, he was seeing an elderly woman suffering from untreatable angina. She discussed with her doctor not only the medical realities of her condition but her own spiritual beliefs that sustained her in her illness. She testified to the power of prayer in her life and the assurance of God's love and care, whether she lived or died. When she had shared her faith, she turned to her physician and asked him what he believed. He said he was flushed for a moment and then stammered that he didn't know. But this encounter sent him into study and reflection. He talked with a pastor in town to understand what his patients were experiencing. The pastor provided him with books pertinent to his question. He concluded that as a scientist he had screened out some of the most important data he should have considered, the evidence of people standing up against debilitating illness and death who were yet assured of the love and everlasting mercy of God. Ever the thorough researcher, he determined that the belief and trust he had regarded as crutches were apertures into the reality of God. He concluded that the marvelous mechanism he had researched in the laboratory was evidence of the presence of a mind that pervades the universe. He termed the genome code the "language of God" and resolved that he could worship God both in the laboratory and in the cathedral.[10]

The patients who impressed Dr. Collins so vividly viewed the world as God's creation through a community of faith. Through that community they had been led to participate in worship, study of the Scriptures, personal prayer, care for one another, and other practices commended by their community. No blueprint or formula led them from their experience of pain and awareness of their mortality to their trust in God. What they had learned was confidence in the goodness of God and trust that whether they lived or died, they were the Lord's. That confidence and trust lay deeper than words could express. It was tacit knowledge of God.

Actions as Apertures to Faith

We have observed several references in the Bible to knowing God with our hearts, souls, and strength. This has provided occasion to remember that the role of the heart in knowing and loving God is more than its function as the seat of human emotions. The "heart," as it is used in the Bible, means the whole of our feeling or emotions, our reason, and our will.[11] The call of Jesus to the future disciples was abrupt: "Follow me and I will make you fish for people" (Mark 1:17). There was apparently no orientation. What we hear is just the declaration of the coming of God's kingdom and the call to join him in announcing the kingdom, healing the sick,

---

10 Collins, *The Language of God*, 211 (see chap. 2, n. 1).
11 Gerhard von Rad, *Old Testament Theology*, vol. 1, trans. D. M. G. Stalker (New York: Harper & Row, 1962), 153.

befriending those who were isolated and alone, and calling their hearers to repentance and faith. In the first three Gospels, the focus is on a disciple's decision to heed Jesus's call. Only later, as Jesus faced the necessity to go to Jerusalem and be crucified, did he raise the question of his own identity. Only then could Peter answer directly that Jesus was the Messiah (Mark 8:29). The disclosure of Jesus as Messiah came *after* Peter's decision to follow and not as a precondition.

In all our knowing, as we have said, we are intermixtures of thinking, feeling, and willing creatures. It is true that occasionally one of those three functions will predominate, but any action of the self involves an element of each. Any one of those three functions of the self may provide an avenue for embodying faith. We often assume that in matters of faith we first decide with our minds and on this basis follow this conclusion with commitment and devotion of the self. This may be the sequence for some. But we have to recognize that for some the route to a changed perspective on life may follow a pathway through action and an orientation of the will. In the previous reference to Sara Miles, her conversion came about through participation in a welcoming community and a decision to provide food for people who needed it. In an earlier revival tradition in this country, so powerful in the founding and growth of the church in parts of this country, the first step of faith was the decision to go forward and commit one's life to Christ. In so doing, this individual action was a sign and declaration before friends and neighbors of a basic decision, a commitment to walk in a new way.

One aphorism holds that we are more likely to act our way into new ways of thinking than we are to think our way into new ways of acting.[12] Community organizers seeking to introduce change into a community may work with the community to select one concrete issue for action and change. Perhaps it is the need for a traffic light or removal of an abandoned and decaying house from the community. The process of organizing and acting for change helps the community see itself in a different light. It also helps community members to understand the forces that have power to resist change. To succeed in a relatively minor matter will help the community to see themselves no longer as helpless victims but as potent forces in the neighborhood. Deciding to act may be the first step in seeing one's community and one's role in it in an entirely different light.

> Faith is a decision of fundamental
> trust and a new perception.

When Mrs. Rosa Parks refused to go to the back of the bus because she was African-American, her refusal to accede to demands of racial segregation was not only an act of civil disobedience but a declaration of her understanding of her identity as a child of God and what God's justice required in the situation. Theologian Heinrich Ott accurately observed, "When a person dares to live on the basis of the unseen, to draw strength and standards not from the visible world, but from the invisible reality of God, to focus on a word of promise (the Gospel of Christ), then he or she achieves a new perspective. This provides no new

---

12 This is a variation of a saying attributed to Bill Wilson of Alcoholics Anonymous in Australia: "You can't think your way into right action, but you can act your way into right thinking."

information concerning things, but is, as it were, a new vision of reality as a whole."[13]

Faith is both a decision of fundamental trust and a new perception.

Action, Conviction, and Belief

Our contention is that we come to know God through participation in community and in actions that flow from this participation. Through the community of faith we learn to interpret the world in the light of a common story. And it is in the context of sharing in that community and interpreting the world through its story that we experience who God is. It is not that we first settle all our questions about ultimate reality and then seek out a community that shares them. Convictions about ultimate reality are linked to and rooted in the experience of being in a community and learning the practices associated with that community.

The words we use take on their meaning by a context. If we use the word *bark*, it makes a difference whether we are speaking about the surface of a tree trunk or the sound made by a dog. The context of the sentence or conversation helps to understand its meaning. At the extremities of human life, our life is given its meaning through our ultimate context or, as sociologist Robert Wuthnow expresses it, "some form of holistic or transcendent symbol system that embraces all of life."[14] This symbol system

---

13 Quoted in Robert A. Evans and Thomas D. Parker, eds., *Christian Theology: A Case Method Approach* (New York: Harper & Row, 1976), 47.

14 Robert Wuthnow, *Christianity in the 21st Century: Reflections on the Challenges Ahead* (New York: Oxford University Press, 1993), 100.

addresses questions such as: Where did I come from? For what am I living? What happens when I die? In wider scope the ultimate context includes such questions as: What is the good life? and, Where is humanity headed? Questions such as these are sometimes addressed by philosophical systems elaborately drawn to explain ultimate reality or creedal systems. It is more typical, however, to address such questions implicitly by parables and stories that provide a context for answering them.[15]

This raises the question of how these convictions or beliefs that provide context for our lives are formed. Traditionally, shaping our convictions about God and faith has been considered an individual effort. We thought that each individual, considering evidence that cannot be denied, forms convictions that represent ultimate reality—the way things are. Today there are serious challenges to such an individualistic assumption. Several voices insist that we see the world not as isolated individuals but as members of interpretive communities. Narratives shared by these communities help shape the way we view the world. The language we use to describe ultimate reality issues forth from the experience of a community of faith, the practices implicit in that community, its worship, its moral insights, and its witness in the world.[16] The historical tradition in which the church stands refers to narratives or events in which the church has experienced the presence of God. It was at such points, wrote theologian Reinhold Niebuhr, that human wisdom and goodness met their limits and that people of faith encountered

---

15 Ibid., 100–101.
16 Murphy, "Bridging Theology and Science in a Postmodern Age," 45 (see chap. 8, n. 6).

the wisdom of God. "Once faith is induced it becomes truly the wisdom that makes 'sense' out of a life and history which would otherwise remain senseless."[17] We are reminded that Saint Paul, in writing to the Christians at Corinth, said that they did not discover God in the elaborate arguments of the rhetoricians and debaters of the age: "For since, in the wisdom of God, the world did not know God through wisdom, God decided, through the foolishness of our proclamation, to save those who believe" (1 Corinthians 1:21).

The use of the experience of the Christian community as a starting point is not an argument against use of our intelligence in knowing God. It is to suggest that we know elements of experience in a means appropriate to those particular elements. We know physical events through observation and measurement. We know other people through communication and action with them. And we know God, who is the context for all our knowing, through events in which a community has experienced the divine presence.

There is thus a certain indirectness in how we may know God. It is true that in experience we believe we encounter God in our own lives. But our encounter is never at the same level we encounter individual elements in our world. Our understanding of God is what we need to declare in order to make sense, as Niebuhr said, of what we have experienced.

Every proposition about the world refers to some body of experience. The experience to which Christian beliefs refer is that of the Christian community in its history, and this history helps us interpret the present. Propositions refined into doctrines undergo

---

17 Reinhold Niebuhr, *The Nature and Destiny of Man* (New York: Charles Scribner's Sons, 1945), 2:206.

change in the light of the experience of successive generations, because they refer to God in our midst now. We can be assured that the formulation of human minds can never fully comprehend the reality to which they refer, but they point us in the direction of God and serve as signposts in walking in a Christian path. They help us see beyond sight into deeper and grander realities. They help us take steps on what otherwise appears to be uncertain ground. "The pulse of certainty," wrote theologian John Baillie, "beats throughout the whole of our Christian knowledge, but we can never quite capture it in our formulations."[18]

The aim of Christian belief or doctrine is not to complete a speculative depiction of a detached realm of reality apart from our everyday life. Christian belief arises out of Christian practice and is intended to guide our action. John Baillie contended that "no doctrine has right of place within our Christian theology unless we can show that the denial of it would disturb or distort that pattern of our Christian sharing in . . . relationships between the triune God, ourselves and our fellows."[19] The body of Christian beliefs is intended to gather up, critically examine, and declare what the Christian community experiences.

In Christian thought we examine the implications of our faith for their consistency with one another and their intelligible fit with all that we know about life and the world through other means. If correct, as Niebuhr said, they should "make sense" out of life and history that would otherwise remain senseless. At this point

---

18 John Baillie, *The Sense of the Presence of God* (New York: Charles Scribner's Sons, 1962), 161.
19 Ibid., 153.

it is appropriate to refer back to chapter 8, titled "Faith Seeking Explanation." In our discussion of faith and science, I suggested that various findings of science about the world (e.g., that it had a beginning, that various levels of life emerge from preceding levels, that a number of variables meet incredibly demanding requirements in order for human life to emerge) are understandable if the world, as faith affirms, is suffused with the mind and intelligence of a divine creator. John Polkinghorne holds that the ability to understand the world is a gift of the Creator. "Through the exercise of this gift," he says, "those working in fundamental physics are able to discern a world of deep and beautiful order—a universe shot through with signs of mind." And he concludes, "I believe that it is indeed the Mind of the world's Creator that is perceived in this way. Science is possible because the universe is a divine creation."[20]

We return, however, to the question about the standing of our beliefs about God. We have held here that they grow out of the practices and life of a community in history. What we believe grows out of our historical experience as it is embraced, critically examined, and refined by each generation. These beliefs are intended to guide the practice of the community and not primarily to satisfy our curiosity about the world. Sometimes those statements became rather speculative and somewhat detached, but at their origin and in their survival, they were deemed essential for guiding the Christian community in its action.[21] Thus Christian beliefs grow out of practice and refer back to service as a guide to

---

20 Polkinghorne, *Quantum Physics and Theology*, 8 (see chap. 3, n. 21).
21 See ibid., 165–66.

Christian action and practice. But even when we can't make sense of the world, we walk in faith because of the Christians who walk with us now and have walked before us.

In practical terms we could refer to one of the first major debates and discussions for the church in forming its belief—the Trinity and the person of Christ. The Christian community arose from Jewish soil, and it grew and remained true to the Jewish community's belief in one God. This one true God, they affirmed, was alone worthy of their worship. Yet, as we saw in chapter 6, they were led to render devotion to Jesus Christ without for a moment retreating from their belief that God is one. The only way they could reconcile their experience and action was to understand that in doing devotion to Christ they were also worshipping God. Furthermore, after Pentecost, they experienced a Presence with them, a Spirit, who guided them in the spread of the church throughout the Mediterranean world. The question that confronted them, then, was how to interpret the experience of one God whose presence they had experienced in three authentic forms. The teachings about the Trinity and the person of Christ were thus efforts to be true to their experience as people of faith. To have referred to Jesus as a "superman" or subdeity would have betrayed what they had actually experienced as a community of faith.

In this context it is fitting to refer once more to parallels between the knowledge of science and that of religion. We noted Michael Polanyi's emphasis on tacit knowledge, knowing more than we can put into words. His examples were learning to ride a bike or to swim by utilizing forces that we have not fully identified or articulated. We recognize a friend's face, he reminded us, without enumerating exactly how it is that we identify him or her. We learn grammar so that we can use it effortlessly and implicitly as a tool of effective expression. Knowledge in any of these endeavors is likely of little use to us until it has become practical knowledge, tacit knowledge that we do not so much analyze but embody and employ. Tacit knowledge thus becomes an extension of ourselves, indispensable for our functioning.[22]

Tacit or implicit knowledge is also employed in Christian belief and action. In Christian life we act on and know more than we can say. We experience more about love, mercy, forgiveness, reconciliation, and justice than we can express in words. The patients Dr. Collins encountered learned through worship, prayer, and service about realities they could see but could not reduce to abstract thought. When they were confronted by pain, need, or the prospect of death, they employed and relied on sources of strength that gave them bearing and direction. That tacit knowledge, operating as naturally as swimming, guided their conduct in difficult times.

C. S. Lewis spoke of Christian worship in a similar manner. He said that when you worship, receive the sacraments, repent, or intercede, it is best if you don't have to think about it. Your thought is focused on God and not on the manner in which you are reaching toward God. He suggests that as long as you have to count the steps, you are really not dancing; you're just learning to dance. "The perfect church service would be the one we were almost unaware of; our attention would have been on God." It is for this

---

22 From Michael Polanyi, *Knowing and Being* (London, 1969), summarized in Armstrong, *The Case for God,* 285 (see chap. 4, n. 2).

reason he resisted endless innovation in worship: "I can make do with almost any kind of service whatsoever," he said, "if only it will stay put." He considered our presence before God in worship as a "trained habit."[23]

Since Christian doctrine and beliefs are more adequately understood as practical knowledge rather than a purely speculative system, it is useful to think of doctrine as a map. When we are taking a trip, a map is not a replacement for what we will see. It is a guide showing way markers to direct us to where we want to go. Its function is not to serve as a substitute for going there but to delineate the route that will lead us to attain the goal we set out to reach. Christian convictions and beliefs grow out of the action of a community of faith. They are confirmed by the way they fit with and guide that action in the future.

REFLECTION QUESTIONS

1. What practices of Christian faith are most conducive to knowing God? What does it mean to you to say that Christian practices are worth doing for their own sake?

2. In what way can we say that practices enable us to know more than we can say? How would practices such as prayer, worship, acts of compassion, and reconciling differences between individuals disclose truth we are unable fully to reduce to words?

---

23 C. S. Lewis, *Letters to Malcolm*, in Lewis's *The Joyful Christian* (New York: Macmillan, 1977), 80–81.

3. Has anyone you know acted his or her way into a new mind-set or outlook on life? How did that happen? How do you understand the experience of Sara Miles in coming to Christian faith?

4. How does discussion of Christian practices help in understanding the connection between acts of devotion such as prayer and worship, on the one hand, and acts of compassion and reconciliation on the other? Do both kinds of practice bring us closer to God?

5. How do you understand Christian practices as channels of grace? How are they habitations of the Spirit?

6. Do you believe that certain teachings or beliefs are closely linked with how we live our lives? How do our convictions about God relate to our attitudes and actions toward others?

A Deeper Way of Seeing

For now we see in a mirror,
dimly, but then we will see face to face.
Now I know only in part; then I will know fully,
even as I have been fully known.

—1 Corinthians 13:12

We began this book with words from George Eliot's preacher, Dinah, telling her congregation, "We are in sad want of good news about God." And she continued, "For everything else comes to an end and when we die we shall leave it all, but God lasts when everything else is gone." As if he were giving a hearty "amen" to Dinah, we heard physicist Marcelo Gleiser hold that our challenge rests in our finite life span, "the fact that our bodies perish in time. . . . We exist in time, whereas God exists without."[1] The quest for a unified theory of the fundamental forces in the universe, Gleiser says, is also "the passionate pursuit of something much larger than ourselves, something timeless, universal,

---

1   Gleiser, *The Prophet and the Astronomer*, 234 (see chap. 1, n. 5).

all-determining." Acknowledging that such a position might cause some of his atheistic high-energy physicist friends to "cringe," he asked them to "consider the notion that we live within time and yearn to transcend it."[2]

Whether in twenty-first-century high-energy physics or nineteenth-century field preaching, amid constant change, humanity still seeks "what lasts when everything else is gone." Or, in Alfred North Whitehead's words, we want "something that stands beyond, behind, and within, the passing flux of immediate things."[3] Coming to know and have faith in God is learning to see the ultimate in the immediate, to discern the enduring in the transience of life.

Learning to See

A central contention throughout our discussion is that religion and science view the same world. The realm of religious faith is not separate from the world of science. Rather, it is a deeper and more comprehensive way of seeing the world that is shared by both. We should expect, therefore, that the two ventures, religion and science, should complement rather than collide with one another. It is the same world, a world that religious faith understands as God's creation. If this is true, there is every reason to expect that the knowledge yielded by scientific research will enhance our efforts to grasp the grandeur of God.

---

2   Ibid.

3   Whitehead, *Science and the Modern World*, in Ramsey, *Christian Discourse*, 66 (see chap. 1, n. 4).

Truths in either science or religion do not come prepackaged and predigested, because all that we know is repeatedly interpreted. We interpret what we see and experience within a framework of what we believe the world is like. In science this scaffolding is called a *theory.* In religion that framework is a comprehensive story incorporating events believed to be particularly transparent to Ultimate Reality, God. Christians find the center and criteria for that disclosure in the life, death, and resurrection of Jesus Christ.

A Parable on Learning to See

A field report from anthropologist Colin Turnbull provides what we can take as a parable on the operation of faith in our interaction with the world. Turnbull lived for three years with the Mbuti community in the Ituri equatorial rain forest that stretches for thousands of square miles in what is now the Republic of Congo in central Africa. His report on the community in which he lived was not written strictly in the style of a technical treatise. Rather, he wrote about the lives of the community in which he lived as friends and neighbors and not merely as subjects in a sociological study. Over the years the Mbuti community looked on him in similar terms. He even received the facial markings that designated him as a member of their tribe. His adopted community, referred to as the forest people, made their home in a small area hacked out of the surrounding rain forest. So thick was the forestation that surrounded them that they never saw objects more than a few yards in the distance. The sun scarcely penetrated the dense canopy of leaves. Hunters walked single file along animal tracks in the forest. Though the Mbuti hunters were short in stature, they often had to bend down as they walked in order to duck under the vegetation that rapidly closed in the paths. Their livelihood was the yield of game, berries, mushrooms, fruit, and other products of the forest.

On one occasion Turnbull invited one of his friends, Kenge, to join him for a journey to the world outside. This was the first time Kenge had ever ventured beyond his forest home. After driving through mountains along narrow dirt roads, their odyssey took them to a high promontory overlooking an expanse of open fields and plains. From their lofty location they saw animals grazing in the distance. Turn-bull's friend struggled to take in the view, and he expressed shock that this area was populated by tiny animals. They appeared to him as small copies of the animals he saw at home. They could not be real, he claimed. At one point he saw on a hillside more than a mile in the distance a mass of "insects," and he urged Turnbull to explain what kind of strange insects he was seeing. Turnbull assured him that they were not insects but buffaloes, just like the ones he had seen crushing through the forest at home. As they drove down from the peak, the "insects" that Kenge saw grew larger, and he asked that they close the windows of their jeep. Clearly upset by this confusing world, Kenge insisted that they leave the area quickly and get back home where the animals were of normal size.

Turnbull realized then that nothing in his friend's experience had helped him to see objects from a distance and to adjust his estimates of size accordingly. Lacking such, he viewed what was clearly before him as insubstantial, menacing, and unreal.

He confronted a new world equipped only with an imagination shaped by the constrictions of his home hewn from the forest.[4]

There is a prevalent temptation to regard only a narrow enclave of experience hewn out of human life as real and knowable. That constricted area of experience is the sphere of things we can see and touch. Anything beyond sense experience is regarded as merely subjective, not knowledge. It is relegated by some to the realm of the fanciful and unreal, and it is reduced or reinterpreted to what we can measure and define. For example, some are committed to interpreting all human conduct from the point of view of base, selfish motives. In their view what some may interpret as altruism is really more accurately a reflection of a desire to pass on one's genes to an oncoming generation, an effort to defend one's kinship group, or some other such self-centered motivation. Having decided ahead of the facts that there is no realm of values to which we are account-able, these reductionists must interpret all that they see in human conduct from a constricted and, in their estimation, valueless point of view. Since they have formed their understanding of the world from this narrowed perspective, realities of human life that seem to abide in grander scale are dismissed as delusional, pathological, fanciful, and unreal. Recall the aphorism of Albert Einstein: "Whether you can observe a thing or not depends on the theory which you use. It is the theory which determines what can be observed."[5]

We insist that the inability to interpret something within prevailing mental models should not be counted as evidence that it

---

4   Colin M. Turnbull, *The Forest People* (New York: Simon & Schuster, 1962), chap. 14.

5   Quoted in Salam, *Unification of Fundamental Forces* (see chap. 1, n. 13).

does not exist. This would be like interpreting a distant herd of buffalo as a swarm of insects. The denial of any experience of God is not proof that God is not there. It is a consequence of a prior decision on the part of the observer, one that cannot be proved, that the world is "self-existent, self-explanatory, self-operating, and self-directing"[6] Severely limiting the definition of the real, these observers lack the interpretive capacity to see the fullness and truth of a world as it exists.

The premise of this book is that faith can be understood, in part, as a way of seeing the world more deeply. Jesus did not engage in long deliberations on theological topics. He helped his hearers see and so experience the redeeming love of God in the commonplace. The joy of God in welcoming the sinners and disinherited was seen in the elation of a widow in finding the coin she had lost (Luke 15:8-10). The generous grace of God was shown in the story of the vineyard owner who voluntarily paid a whole day's wage to workers who worked only the last hour of the day (Matthew 20:1-16). The redeeming love of God was disclosed in the story of a shepherd who left his flock to find the one sheep out of a hundred that was lost (Matthew 18:12-14). The parables were tools of teaching that helped hearers see the world around in a new and deeper dimension—to see the ultimate in the immediate.

Saint Paul intentionally used the model of vision to speak about how we know God. He told his churches that what they now saw only in part would be fully disclosed in the time to come. People in the congregation in Corinth prized and cultivated many ways of

---

6   From a definition of "naturalism" in Dagobert D. Runes, ed., *The Dictionary of Philosophy* (New York: Philosophical Library), 1942.

knowing God. Some spoke in tongues. Others showed prophetic powers or great wisdom. Many sacrificed and gave generously to others. All these gifts—and others—yield only a partial vision of who God is. Now, Paul reminded them, we see in part like puzzling reflections in a mirror, but in the time to come we will see "face to face" (1 Corinthians 13:12). Until that day there are three gifts that guide us in knowing God. They are faith, hope, and love. And the greatest of them is love (v. 13).

Perhaps we can understand the function of these three gifts described by Paul—faith, hope, and love—by an analogy to the way we see the world around us. Those who study human vision remind us that we see at least as much with our brains as we do with our eyes. An eye surgeon alerted patients who were to receive new advanced-technology implanted lenses following their cataract surgery that they should not expect the full benefits of their new lenses immediately. Time is required, he advised, for the brain to learn how to interpret the information now available through the implanted lenses. Behind his advice to patients was his knowledge that an elaborate set of mechanisms make it possible for a person to register what is before him. Photoreceptor cells in the retina process light into electromagnetic signals that are conducted by the optic nerve via the thalamus in the brain to the cerebral cortex, where we perceive. The cerebral cortex stores categories and concepts from all that we have learned and experienced, and those categories and concepts help the brain to transform electromagnetic signals into sight.

We are reminded of the active role of the brain and our emotions in seeing our world when we find ourselves, sometimes out of fear or excitement, "seeing" objects or figures that are either not there at all or are badly misinterpreted. A stretch of highway under bright sunlight may appear to us as a body of water. A bush or other object beside a footpath at dusk may be interpreted as a lurking threat. Kenge had not had the opportunity to learn how to interpret the size of objects viewed from a distance, so it was natural for him to report seeing objects using the only frame of reference known to him in his forest home. Our eyes direct signals to the brain; but it is our brains, using concepts formed by experience, that make it possible for us to see and know what we see.

There are parallels between the role of the brain in vision and the functioning of faith, hope, and love in coming to know God. Just as the brain shapes what we see, the gifts of faith, hope, and love help shape us to sense the presence and leading of God. There is likely no experience that will bear a large sign saying, "This is God." But the expectations shaped by faith, hope, and love help us sense God's presence in our lives. Thus, an urge to help a neighbor, to take a stand for justice in our community, or to be an agent of reconciliation may be interpreted in the eyes of faith as the calling of God. Faith, hope, and love are gifts that discern and interpret that calling and presence in our lives.

Faith

"Now faith is the assurance of things hoped for, the conviction of things not seen" (Hebrews 11:1). Faith not only serves as a foundation for the present; it provides assurance that what we now hold in trust will finally be confirmed by sight. When we become people of faith, we come to understand ourselves and to view the story of our lives as it is illuminated and embedded in the larger story of

God's dealings with the world. We anchor our lives and our destiny in the divine reality disclosed in the stories of faith and claim the promises contained within them as our own. We acknowledge that this larger sweep of history is now known only partially, but we are rock solid in our expectation that we will one day see face-to-face.

Faith is a gift that gives meaning and direction to history and our journey within it. Life and history are sometimes viewed through the quiet resignation of the book of Ecclesiastes, in which "the Teacher" reflects: "What has been is what will be, / and what has been done is what will be done; / there is nothing new under the sun" (1:9). Life in this perspective is a cycle of endless repetition. We exit at the same point we came in. But the prevailing conviction of the Bible is that history is headed toward a goal—to the realization of the divine purpose. In the daunting years of World War II, Christian theologian Reinhold Niebuhr reminded his generation that history is transformed when a Christ, a Messiah, is expected. Historical events are seen not as a repetition of what has always been but as points on a journey of history in which God is involved.[7] The stories of the Bible reflect that God has purposes in history and that these purposes will prevail regardless of fears and dreads that imply the opposite. In the sway of those narratives the world has meaning and possibilities that deliver human life from futility and decay. The novelist Cynthia Ozick testifies to the manner in which faith illuminates history and the world in which we live: "For novelists it matters very much whether the Messiah has come or is yet to come. The human difference is this: If the

---

7   Reinhold Niebuhr in the Gifford Lectures, *The Nature and Destiny of Man*, vol. 2, chap. 1 (see chap. 10, n. 17).

Messiah has not yet appeared, then the world is still profane, and our task is to wrest him forth. . . . But if the Messiah has already cleft the skin of human history, then the world is at that moment transfigured into a holy site."[8]

A Deeper Way of Seeing

We need to understand faith, therefore, as a means of seeing more deeply the significance of the events through which we pass. We see glimpses of God's reign, Jesus said, just by observing the world with the eyes of faith. We see God at work in the lilies growing freely in the field. We see illustrations of God's provident care for the creation in observing the seed thrusting through the soil and producing food, in generosity to a neighbor's need, or in returning the lost to the fold. Faith in this sense is a gift of discerning the more profound significance of occurrences at hand.

The twentieth-century theologian John Baillie spoke in his Gifford lectures of "the sense of the presence of God." He reminded his hearers that we develop sensitivities that go beyond the purview of the bodily senses. We speak, for example, of common sense, a sense of beauty, a sense of right and wrong, and even a sense of humor. All of these ways of perceiving a situation represent a refinement of sensibilities that make it possible for us to discern elements in an experience that go beyond the realm of what we can see and touch.[9] Some, for example, will be more finely tuned than others to the sensitivities and feelings of other people and will know instinctively how another person is feeling. Specialists in music will

---

8   Cynthia Ozick, quoted in John B. Cobb Jr., *Liberal Christianity at the Crossroads* (Philadelphia: Westminster Press, 1973), 125.

9   Baillie, *The Sense of the Presence of God*, 52–53 (see chap. 10, n. 18).

hear subtle dimensions of a musical composition that will be missed by many of the rest of us. A person lacking a sense of humor will hear the same joke as another and fail to hear anything funny about it. A person with a sense of humor may laugh uproariously at a good joke but find himself incapable of stirring a similar response from a humorless friend who doesn't get the point.

> People of faith experience the same events as others but experience a deeper sense of perception.

Perhaps we can understand our experience of God in faith as an analogy to a sense of humor or to common sense. It is similar in that the person of faith is exposed to the same events as another, but he or she experiences them in their depth. Maybe others saw the bush Moses saw, but only he saw that it was burning but not consumed, and he took off his shoes to acknowledge he was standing on holy ground (Exodus 3:1-6). An acquired sense of depth allows us to interpret the size of objects viewed from a distance. In a similar manner, faith that is lived and refined helps us see the depth of meaning in daily events.

The Search for Depth

This search for depth, the quest for what lasts when everything else is gone, is interwoven in all we experience, whether acknowledged or not. In the impulse of humans to reach out for a wider context, we experience the stirrings of God. In East Germany, under an atheistic regime before the reunification of Germany, graffiti on a wall read, "Find me a God, for I am full of prayer." Sensing the presence of God may be as much action as it is reflection. Perhaps it is as apt to say that we believe because we pray as it is to say that we pray because we believe. We experience a similar impulse in response to the sheer beauty and grandeur of life. One woman on witnessing a scene of breathtaking beauty said, "Oh, if I could only make a sound of praise to someone!" We sense the presence of God in our need to exult in praise.

Seeing God in the World

Faith leads to communion with God. Faith helps us grasp the world as an arena in which the Messiah has appeared. Faith comprehends the world through the perspective of a story in which God is working out the divine purpose in our midst. God is seen behind, before, and within the world and our lives. The same God whose majesty and mind are shown in billions of galaxies and stars, including our sun, is shown as well in the exquisite structures of subatomic physics.

Theologian John Cobb speaks of God as the One who calls the world forward. This call of God is observed even in the cellular structure of our bodies. When we pray for healing for ourselves and others, Cobb suggests, we are seeking to cooperate with God's call forward in every cell for God's purposes of healing and wholeness.[10]

Experiencing God in Christian Practices

The practices of Christian faith are well-worn pathways by which people of faith sense the presence of God in our common life. We

---

10 John Cobb, *Jesus' Abba: The God Who Has Not Failed* (Minneapolis: Fortress Press, 2015), 68–69.

speak of these practices as "habitations of the Spirit" and channels of God's grace. In engaging in Christian practices, we put faith into action. In the experience of prayer and praise, in fellowship with other Christians, in acts of mercy and justice, and in sharing of resources, we experience firsthand the love and grace of God. We learn to position our lives in certain ways that lead us to communion with God. That communion can take shape in public worship in which we praise God as the One above all who is worthy of our praise and devotion. It can take place as well in prayer for others, in offering food to the hungry, in providing companionship with those who alone or in working for justice for those who are the disinherited, dispossessed in our world.

Particular Disclosures of God

There are moments in the lives of many people of faith when they sense that they have experienced the presence of God in an unusually direct manner. For some it may have appeared in an overwhelming flood of joy and fulfillment. For others it may have been a sense of deliverance or pardon. For yet others it may come in the form of the courage and power to live through overwhelming loss and devastation. These singular occasions may have come in moments of private prayer or in public worship. We can be grateful if we have experienced such events in our own lives. They serve as signposts in our faith to which we may refer for inspiration and guidance. Yet we should not despair in the thought that these exceptional moments are the only or even the most typical ways in which we know God. While such epiphanies are welcome apertures into the divine, we should not suppose that the lack of them signifies that our lives must or can be lived in the absence of the divine. John Cobb reminds us that Jesus himself did not talk at length about these special experiences or teach his hearers to seek them for themselves. But we do not doubt that God is involved in them.[11]

> Even in the most desperate circumstances,
> God is working to accomplish the divine purposes.

Saint Paul, in writing to the Romans, did not promise that all things will be tranquil and pleasant. Yet he insisted that even in the most desperate circumstances, God is working to accomplish the divine purposes. The Revised Standard Version expresses it this way: "We know that in everything God works for good with those who love him" (Romans 8:28). Later in the same chapter, he affirms that none of the threats that we fear—life and death, political rulers, things present or things to come—none of them will be able to separate us from the love of God in Jesus Christ (vv. 38-39).

The life of faith enables us to see with new eyes the passages of exaltation and anguish through which all flesh must pass. The late Arthur Peacocke was a professor of physical biochemistry at Birmingham and Oxford universities, as well as a professor of theology at Clare College, Cambridge. He authored a number of books in both scientific research and in theology. After a long life of research and teaching, he was diagnosed with an advanced case of prostate cancer. In coming to terms with this new reality in his life, he reported that he experienced what he had long thought to be the significance of intercessory prayer. He had believed, he

---

11   Ibid., 48.

said, that when one prays for another, the one who prays places himself or herself in the presence of God and enables the person on whose behalf he prays to experience the "enfolding presence of God." He found this assuredly true in his experience as he was surrounded by prayers on his behalf from family, friends, and colleagues. He was fortified further in the assurance and the absolute conviction that "God is love and eternally so." The foundation for his prayers, he reported, was the affirmation that "underneath are the everlasting arms."[12]

Peacocke's research and writings had included discussions of natural evil. He argued in his publications that what we term "natural evil" is a result of a divinely created structure of natural law that fulfills God's purpose of creating intelligent persons. He illustrated this contention by citing the role played by mutations in DNA in evolution and thus in the emergence of human beings. It was ironic, he noted, that these mutations in DNA were also the basic source of the cancer that was ending his life. He testified that he was able to meet the challenge because of his trust in the love and goodness of God. He was sustained, he said, by his "root conviction that God is Love as revealed supremely in the life, death, and resurrection of Jesus the Christ."[13] An abiding faith provides a way of seeing the ultimate amid suffering as well as in joy.

In the parable with which we began this chapter, Turnbull's friend and fellow traveler in the Republic of Congo faced a world for which nothing in his experience had prepared him. He lacked

---

12 Arthur Peacocke, *All That Is: A Naturalistic Faith for the Twenty-First Century* (Minneapolis: Fortress Press, 2007), 192.
13 Ibid., 192–93.

the capacity to interpret the distant view. Faith, much like our ability to gauge the size of objects seen from afar, is a cultivated, a practiced means of interpretation. It equips us to grasp the vastness of God's love and providence within the scope of our present experience. Faith widens our otherwise constricted surroundings and helps us interpret life both in its immediate and in its ultimate dimensions. It shapes the world in which we live into a holy site and delivers it from futility and death.

Hope

If faith both interprets the present and looks expectantly to the time to come, hope makes that future reference emphatic. Earlier we recalled that faith, according to the Letter to the Hebrews, "is the assurance of things hoped for, the conviction of things not seen" (11:1). The assurance (*upostasis*) of which the book of Hebrews speaks is a base or foundation (the literal meaning of the Greek term) for the time to come. The same Greek term can also be used to refer to a title or deed for property. Thus, faith forms the foundation for hope in the future. It gives focus to the conviction that God is behind, beyond, and within the world, working for good in all things, and that God's good purposes will ultimately prevail.

Hope is faith translated into time. Having experienced through faith God's redemptive love in the present, we count on God's faithfulness in the time to come. God's purposes, we believe, may be relied on whether we wake or sleep (1 Thessalonians 5:9-10). Faith and hope are correlated and unified as expressions of confidence and trust in the Ultimate Reality surrounding our lives—God. In flourishing times it is easy to be optimistic. We think that life is within our control and that we have the means to address any obstacles we confront. But hope thrives even or especially when we think we have run out of possibilities. Hope is not dependent on promising prospects. In Bill Coffin's words, "Hope needs to be understood as a reflection of the state of your soul, not a reflection of the circumstances that surround your days."[14]

{ **Hope is faith translated into time.** }

In the first three Gospels of the New Testament, Jesus speaks of the realm fulfilling God's will as the kingdom of God. It is the state of affairs in which God's will is done. In Jesus's teaching that gracious reign of God is both present in our midst and yet to come. Once again, the parables that were Jesus's principal way of teaching provide us with glimpses or foretastes of what God's righteous rule is like when it appears. The sick are healed, the outcasts are brought into the human family, those far-off are brought near, and the poor and excluded hear good news preached to them. Human hopes, then, may be invested in this coming righteous reign of God in the affairs of the world.

In John's Gospel, the evangelist spoke more of "eternal life" as our abiding place and the realm of our communion with God. On seventeen occasions, John's Gospel refers to our hope as "eternal life," and there are an additional six such references in the first letter of John. Like the kingdom of God, eternal life is

---

14 William Sloane Coffin, "Raging against Boredom," in *The Life of Meaning: Reflections on Faith, Doubt, and Repairing the World*, ed. Bob Abernathy and William Bole (New York: Seven Stories Press, 2007), 424.

a quality of life that is known in the present and is uninterrupted by death. The heart of the matter is not duration but rather the depth of our relationship with God. It is life in the "age to come" that is available now.

The Letter to the Hebrews acknowledges that this hope, while it is certified and assured in faith, remains yet to be fulfilled. When Hebrews chapter 11 lists an honor roll of faith through biblical history, the author refers to faithful men and women of the past who did not have in hand all that was promised (v. 13). Yet their eyes were fixed on it. They were thus pilgrims on the march. They were aliens and strangers to all in the present world that contradicted God's rule. These people of faith, anchored in hope, were "seeking a homeland" (v. 14). They clung to hope. "Therefore, God is not ashamed to be called their God; indeed he has prepared a city for them" (v. 16).

Vision

People of hope have set their eyes and minds on a destination. They have viewed the future with faith, and though not all that they hope for is within their grasp, they are able to see and greet the promise from afar (11:13). They are homesick for the future and seek a homeland (v. 14). They desire a better country (v. 16). Their expectation of what God will do far exceeds what is now in hand, but they walk on toward the distant goal, confident that God will fulfill the promise in the time to come.

Disaffiliation with the Present

The Old Testament saints' vision as men and women of faith gave birth in them a sense of dissatisfaction with and disaffiliation from the way things were. They yearned for something better. "They confessed that they were strangers and foreigners on the earth" (11:13). There would have been opportunity, we are assured, for them to make their peace with the present state of affairs, but their hope was fixed on a better country. This disaffiliation, this dissatisfaction, married as it was with a vivid sense of God's future, provided robust motivation for struggling for justice and peace in this world. The modern-day prophet Dr. Martin Luther King Jr. reflected this unwillingness to accommodate to the ways that mock God's will. In a 1963 university address, Dr. King spoke of "creative maladjustment" and commended it to his hearers: "I never intend to become adjusted to segregation and discrimination. I never intend to become adjusted to religious bigotry. . . . I never intend to adjust myself to the madness of militarism, [to the] self-defeating effects of physical violence."[15]

Commitment to Change

Men and women of faith and hope are committed absolutely to their vision of God's future. Their vision of the future and their consequent disaffiliation with the present means they regard themselves as strangers and aliens in the present. Furthermore, they are absolutely confident that God will fulfill the promise and that God's victory is assured. Therefore, they give themselves absolutely, according to Hebrews, to the homeland God promises.

The author of Hebrews enumerated the testing the saints of old endured and the horrendous obstacles that these people

---

15 Martin Luther King Jr., address at Western Michigan University, December 18, 1963.

of faith encountered. They "shut the mouth of lions, quenched raging fire, escaped the edge of the sword, won strength out of weakness . . ." (11:33-34). The paragraph that follows cites the trials through which they passed that illustrate their utter faithfulness and hope based on faith. We are to gather from this account that they persisted against overwhelming odds because they had a vision of God's purposes and the resolute confidence that these purposes would prevail. The message coming forth from this recital of luminous men and women of faith is a summons to comparable faithfulness. Hope gives grounds for focus and constancy in spurning the way things are and joining in the pilgrimage to the heavenly country, to the city that God has prepared (v. 16).

> Therefore, since we are surrounded by so great a cloud of witnesses, let us also lay aside every weight and the sin that clings so closely, and let us run with perseverance the race that is set before us, looking to Jesus the pioneer and perfecter of our faith. (12:1-2)

Communion with God

In sharing the vision, in disowning all within the present that betrayed that vision and in committing themselves unreservedly to it, the saints of old came to know God and to live in communion with God. God, we are told, is "not ashamed to be called their God; indeed, he has prepared a city for them" (Hebrews 11:16). They would find no homeland in any realm short of the new city to be built by God. The hope that is fixed on God binds them to the promise.

Because of their hope, they walked with God. Communion with God in hope is not a quiet rest outside the struggles of history. It is pilgrimage toward the promise. They knew God as a force in their history and as a promised homeland at the journey's end.

Love

Faith and hope in New Testament terms are fused with love. In Paul's soaring conclusion to what is sometimes called an "ode to love," he binds together three great gifts in knowing God: "And now faith, hope, and love abide, these three; and the greatest of these is love" (1 Corinthians 13:13). In comparison to all the gifts to be distributed in the church by God's Spirit—tongues, faith, generosity, sacrifice—love abides above all. We now walk by faith, but then we will see God face-to-face. We hope now, but then what we hope for will be ours. It is the very nature of God to love. Love is present when all else has passed away.

Love is the last and most radical step of faith. The deepest measure of love is when we find our welfare in the welfare of the One who loves us. To love God is to confront all that we experience in life, all its joys and pain, and to affirm our trust in the goodness and love of that Ultimate Power who bears us up in life and who will receive us once again. We cited the testimony of scientist and theologian Arthur Peacocke, who acknowledged that the mutations in DNA that were necessary for conscious human life also created the cancer that was soon to end his life. His terminal condition gave added force to his expression of trust in the love of God as shown in Jesus Christ. He closed his testimony with this strong affirmation: "I know that God is waiting for me to be enfolded in love."[16]

{ Love is the last and most radical step of faith. }

Alfred North Whitehead once wrote that religion is the transition from "God the void to God the enemy, and from God the enemy to God the companion."[17] All of us ultimately face limits on our lives. We are brought into life and received once again by a power not our own. Some regard this power as faceless and uncaring, an unseeing force of randomness and might. Others regard this power as a foe, a slayer of all that we value and care for. Yet there are those who find in this ultimate limit on our lives a power of love who knows us by name, who ushers us into life, sustains us on our journey, and receives us again at journey's end. They place their trust—whatever the circumstance—in the goodness and loving direction of this God known to us in Jesus Christ. This is the final step in knowing God.

The biblical authors assure us that in loving God we are simply reflecting the love with which God loves us and the whole creation. We are assured that it is the very nature of God to love. The first letter of John, in enjoining his brothers and sisters to love one another, holds that "love is from God; everyone who loves is born of God and knows God" (1 John 4:7). "No one has ever seen God; if we love one another, God lives in us, and his love is perfected in

16 Peacocke, *All That Is*, 193.

17 Alfred North Whitehead, *Religion in the Making: Lowell Lectures*, repr. ed. (New York: Cambridge University Press, 1926; 2011), 6.

us" (v. 12). Faith and hope speak in future tense about our partial vision yielding to sight and promises leading to fulfillment. Abiding in love lifts us to participate in God now because it is God's very nature to love.

Thus we are not the initiators of love. "We love because he first loved us" (1 John 4:19). If Christian love is finding one's own welfare and good in the welfare of another, that is what commentator Paul Sampley refers to as a circular quality to love. The love of God that redeems and makes us whole cannot be kept to oneself. "It is realized fully only in its being shared with someone else . . . The love of God precedes our responding love, and our love for one another is a reflection of that love."[18] In loving God and in loving one another, we know God and participate in God, because God is love.

Conclusion

We began the discussion of knowing God in this book by referring to our quest for what, or rather, who, lasts. Dinah, the preacher in George Eliot's novel, promised that God lasts when everything else is gone. We saw that many physicists and astronomers hold that the sciences aim for something, as Marcelo Gleiser said, "larger than ourselves, something timeless, universal, all-determining." We spoke of our fleeting attempts to fortify our lives in something beyond ourselves, our possessions, our causes, or even our friends and family. We noted that all these potentially good things, worthy though they are, are themselves destined to come to an end.

---

18 J. Paul Sampley, "Commentary on First Corinthians," The New Interpreter's Bible, vol. X (Nashville: Abingdon Press, 2002), 954–57.

Founding our final security only in what we can procure and possess finally plunges us into futility and despair.

In knowing and loving God, we at last find that which lasts when everything else is gone. When we love God, we can face the reality that the ideals and the people we love will themselves one day perish and pass away. We know that loss is real, but we are persuaded that deeper still is the goodness of the One who brings us into life and receives us once again. Therefore, we can know even in our grief that those we have lost are held in infinite love from which nothing in all creation can separate them. Radical trust in God through Jesus Christ frees us to love others as creatures of God and to rely for our ultimate security on the One who holds us and the whole creation in unfailing love. When we must surrender those we love, and when we breathe our last, we are secure in the trust that underneath us are the everlasting arms.

Seeing God in all things and all things in God is a form of vision cultivated by faith, hope, and love. It opens our spirits to a sphere far beyond the constricted vision of those things we can possess and to which we can cling. It enables us to see the way things are in their widest scope. Faith, hope, and love refract the light of life in our spirits and equip us to sense God in, with, and beyond the world that God has made. Those who love are from God and know God. And the love of God never ends.

REFLECTION QUESTIONS

1.   In what ways do the limitations of a narrowly reductionist scientific stance parallel the restricted vision of a man

who had never journeyed beyond the confines of the rain forest?

2. How do faith, hope, and love function to interpret what we see and experience in a wider experience?

3. Does a sense of humor enable a person to see another world, or is it an added dimension, a deeper way of seeing the same world viewed by those who lack the ability to see humor in what is before them?

4. In what way do you experience hope as an experience that is independent of favorable prospects at hand? How do you respond to Coffin's suggestion that hope is more a reflection of one's soul than of the circumstances around us? What is the difference between hope and optimism?

5. Have you had experiences that confirm the contention that loving God and one another helps us participate in God and know God? In that context, what does it mean to say that "we love because he first loved us" (1 John 4:19)?

6. If loving another means that we find our welfare in the welfare of another, what does it mean to love God? How does loving God affect our relationship to all that is less than God?

Index of Subjects and Authors

Index of Scripture References

CPSIA information can be obtained
at www.ICGtesting.com
Printed in the USA
LVOW10s1359280917
550377LV00001B/6/P